YOUR DEVOTIONAL LIFE DETERMINES YOUR EMOTIONAL LIFE

31 Key Success Plans For Winning Each Day

CRAIG & SAMANTHA JOHNSON

TABLE OF CONTENTS

1

Your Devotional Life Will Determine Your Emotional Life

"But seek first the kingdom of God and his righteousness, and all these things will be added to you" (Matthew 6:33 ESV).

There is a battle going on for control of your mind every day. It's an *epic* fight to control your thoughts, decisions, and actions. If the enemy can control your thoughts and feelings, he can debilitate your mind. The enemy doesn't initially attack your strengths. Rather, he will attack your weaknesses to zap your strength.

The animated Pixar movie "Inside Out" tells the story of five emotions: Anger, Disgust, Fear, Sadness, and Joy. These emotions grapple for control of the mind of an 11-year-old girl named Riley. The movie cleverly illustrates how Riley navigates these emotions daily and how, when they get out of control, these emotions can hurt her and the lives around her. The same is true for us. When you wake up every morning, the enemy sends divisive emotions to fight for control. The main goal is to steal your *joy* and control your thoughts and mind. But there is *hope*! When you start looking for hope to deal with these seemingly never-ending emotions, only one thing is required - sitting at Jesus' feet.

If you are reading this devotional, you are putting Jesus first. Your response, perspective, and view of each day start with who or what you put first. When you put Jesus first, you are allowing the Prince of Peace to take control of your thoughts and emotions; *there,* you will find victory, even amid the storm. The Word of God is the most powerful tool we have. Find devotionals you can read every day. Commit to studying the scriptures. Declare them over your life each morning when you wake up. "I can do all things through Christ who strengthens me" (Philippians 4:13). "The battle is not mine; the battle is the Lords" (2 Chronicles 20:15). "If God is for us, who can be against us" (Romans 8:31).

Pray and listen for God's voice to provide the solutions you need. There is a difference between a *good* idea and a *God* idea. A good idea is where you might say, "I wish I would have thought of that." A God idea is where you would say, "I would have *never* thought of that." We need some "I would have never thought of that" moments on this journey.

Stop fighting the battles meant for God to fight. It's the Mary & Martha principle we see in Luke 10:41-42 where Jesus says to her, "My dear Martha, you are worried and upset over all these details! There is only one thing worth being concerned about. Mary has discovered it, and it will not be taken away from her" (NLT). Jesus didn't come to be served; He came to serve. When you allow Him to serve you, "all of these things will be added to you," as Matthew 6:33 says (NIV). He will give you just what you need when you need it. 2 Corinthians 9:8 promises that "God will generously provide all you need. Then you will always have everything you need, and plenty left over to share with others" (NLT).

When you make the daily choice to put Jesus first in your life, your thoughts will slowly but steadily shift. Your thoughts will eventually move from war to peace, sadness to joy, despair to hope. Every day, make spending time with Jesus your first priority. He will respond and give you all the things you need and more.

I will make a bold statement: The majority of favor I have received in life and ministry has not been due to things I've done, but from the times I have spent with Jesus. He is your ultimate power source. If your desire to *do* more for God is greater than your desire to *spend time* with God, you have a power issue.

Here is the definition of devotion: To show love, loyalty, or enthusiasm for a person, activity, or cause. The question is, what are you devoted to? What do you spend the most time doing? I had to ask myself that question. I found myself spending more time on things in life that were temporal instead of spending time on what would be eternal. When you look at it that way, it changes your perspective. Although, putting God first will help you in the short and long term. Why? Because you are building your relationship with the One who can do it all for you daily.

Daily devotional life will take your relationship with God to a new level. If I compared the favor I had in my life while putting Jesus first to the years I was sporadic in my devotional life, there would be no comparison between the two. God's blessing and favor have been exponential in all facets of my life since making Him a daily priority. When you get up in the morning and put Jesus first place in your life, watch for His goodness to chase you down.

Pray this: Dear God, Your Word says that when I put You first in my life, all of these things will be added. I stand on that promise today. I will not fight my emotions on my own. I will let You fight the battle for me. Amen (So be it).

Declare this: There is *hope* and *grace* for today. I choose to surrender my emotions at the feet of Jesus and trust that He has everything I need. I will see His goodness as I put Him first place in my life. I know that all of His blessings will be added to my life daily!

Win for today: I will give God the first 15 minutes of my day by praying, reading His Word, or meditating on a devotional as I spend time with Him.

2

Peace Is Power

"You will keep in perfect peace all who trust in you, all whose thoughts are fixed on you!" (Isaiah 26:3 NLT).

Every day, you need to fight for peace. This is not a physical or emotional fight but a fight to put yourself in a *position* of peace. Peace is power.

The enemy wants nothing more than to be a peace thief. He works through your emotions to steal what is yours. If you struggle with fear, the emotion of fear will come to highlight what you're most afraid of: failure, being overlooked, or feeling alone. If you deal with disgust, the emotion of disgust emphasizes your mistakes, your appearance, and your feeling of self-worth. If you battle sadness, the emotion of sadness will remind you of your loss, your pain, and your scars. If you deal with anger, the emotion of anger will replay your regrets, your abuse, and your questions of "How could this happen to my child?"

This list could go on and on. But peace is not found in an emotion; it's found in a person. His name is Jesus. He is called the Prince of Peace. When you trust in Jesus and fix your thoughts on Him, you allow the Prince of Peace to calm your mind, lift your spirit, and put you in a position of power. When you have peace of mind, fear and anxiety have to leave. You can stand on the scripture in Psalm 118:6 (NIV) that declares, "The Lord is with me, I will not be afraid. What can mere mortals do to me?" Now, that's powerful!

Remember, God's got this. When people ask for advice on how to make a significant life change, I always tell them to do two things: pray and follow peace. If you don't feel peace in a decision, then wait. You don't have to figure it out on your own. God *will* give you a sense of inner peace, and His way of doing things is always better than ours. When you have peace, you will do things differently than other people. You won't live out of a place of anxiety or fear. You will have peace knowing you are making the right decisions, even if they don't make sense to others.

Some of you have been living on an emotional roller-coaster, allowing your circumstances to determine whether you will be happy. You must put your foot down and say, "That's it. From now on, I'm keeping my peace. I won't allow what's on the outside to get on the inside. I won't keep letting the same people frustrate me or the same circumstances upset me. I'm going to enter into the place of rest."

One way I try to keep my peace is through laughter. Laughter is such an excellent antecedent for peace. I read in an article recently that laughter relaxes the whole body. A good, hearty laugh relieves physical tension and stress, relaxing your muscles for up to 45 minutes. Laughter boosts the immune system. Laughter decreases stress hormones and increases immune cells and infection-fighting antibodies, thus improving your resistance to disease. Laughter triggers the release of endorphins, the body's natural feel-good chemicals. Endorphins promote an overall sense of well-being and can even temporarily relieve pain. Laughter protects the heart. Laughter improves the function of blood vessels and increases blood flow, which can help protect you against a heart attack and other cardiovascular problems. Laughter burns calories. It may be no replacement for going to the gym, but one study found that laughing for 10 to 15 minutes a day can burn approximately 40 calories—enough to lose three or four pounds over a year. Laughter lightens anger's heavy load. Nothing diffuses anger and conflict faster than a shared laugh. Shifting your perspective to see the funny side of a problem enables you to move on from confrontations without holding onto bitterness or resentment. Laughter may even help you to live longer. A study in Norway found that people with a strong sense of humor outlived those who don't laugh as much. The difference was particularly notable for those battling cancer. Laughter is a strong medicine, a prescription to find your peace. When you follow peace, there is a deep knowing that God will cause things to happen that you could never make happen on your own. You can rest in that knowing.

We can't play God and force things to go our way. Life is short, and it's up to you to make it sweet. When you stay in peace, your actions show God you trust Him. Hebrews 4:13 says, "We who believe can enter his rest" (NLT). When we take our hands off a situation, we leave room for God to move. Stay in faith that God is working behind the scenes. Live out of a place of peace and trust.

Remember, when you are in difficult situations, God has people you may not even know about praying for you. He has placed a hedge of protection around you, creating a controlled, safe environment. When you face the enemies of life, declare that they have no control.

God doesn't deliver us from every difficulty, but He will deliver us *through* the difficulty. Quit worrying and losing sleep. God will make a way where there seems to be no way. He is deeply concerned with all that concerns you. Trust Him and live from a place of peace. All day, say, "God's got this!"

Pray this: Dear God, my mind and emotions are fixed on you. What can people do to me? Today, I will put myself in a position of peace by allowing You to work in every area of my life. My trust is in You, Lord. Amen (So be it).

Declare this: I will not let emotions dictate my day. I am in a position of peace. I am strong. I am powerful. Because the Prince of Peace is working on my behalf, I will overcome every obstacle, win every battle, and stay full of peace in every situation.

Win for today: I will find a quiet place and listen for God to speak. Today, I will stay in a place of peace.

3

Reverse

"Now we see things imperfectly, like puzzling reflections in a mirror, but then we will see everything with perfect clarity. All that I know now is partial and incomplete, but then I will know everything completely, just as God now knows me completely" (1 Corinthians 13:12 NLT).

If I could go back to the 80s, I would rethink some of my fashion choices. It's a little embarrassing when I see pictures from those days. You could likely say the same about whatever decade you grew up in. It seemed cool in the moment, but I had no idea how times would change. It's the same in life. We live life forward but understand it in reverse.

Pursue Purpose Over Pleasure

Knowing what I know now, this is what I would tell you: pursue purpose over pleasure. When you pursue pleasure over purpose, you will lose the passion to fulfill your destiny. You'll become lost. Unfulfilled. That's why so many people who have so much are not happy. They will never gain enough pleasure to satisfy their true longing, which is to have purpose. Philippians 4:12-13 says, "I know how to live on almost nothing or with everything. I have learned the secret of living in every situation, whether it is with a full stomach or empty, with plenty or little. For I can do everything through Christ, who gives me strength" (NLT).

You find your purpose through obedience to God's will and plan for your life. As Proverbs 16:9 reminds us, "A man's heart plans his way, but the Lord determines his steps" (HCSB). Success is not an elevator; it's the culmination of every step of obedience you've taken. Your purpose could be at your next step of obedience.

Know Your Identity

Looking in reverse, I would also tell you to know your identity. If you don't know who you are, someone will tell you who they think you *should* be.

I get that we don't like everything about ourselves. We often see someone we admire and want to be like them instead. But God does not copy and paste. He made you extraordinarily unique, full of purpose and destiny. As President Theodore Roosevelt said, "Comparison is the thief of joy." Quit comparing and copying someone else when you're meant to be an original.

Some of us are having an identity crisis. My driver's license says who *I* am. If I tried to be someone else, they would call me a fraud. We don't want to be considered frauds, yet many of us are trying to be someone other than whom God created. The Bible is God's ID. If you want to be like somebody, aspire to be more like Him.

Scripture teaches us both who God is and who God is *to* us. Exodus 3:14 says, "God said to Moses, 'I AM WHO I AM'" (NIV). Whether your challenge today is physical, emotional, or financial, the great I AM declares to you: I AM to you what you need Me to be. Do you need healing? He says, "I am the Lord Who heals you" (Exodus 15:26 NIV). Are you going through a dark time? He says, "I am the light of the world" (John 8:12 NIV). Are you looking for a way out of a bad situation? He says, "I am the Lord your God, your deliverer" (Isaiah 43:3 NET). Are you fearful of the future? He says, "I am the good shepherd" (John 10:11 NIV). Are you confused by people's opinions? He says, "I am the Alpha and Omega, the First and Last, the Beginning and the End" (Revelation 22:13 NIV). God has the final word in your life.

A lack of identity is keeping many people from reaching their full potential. Their minds are full of thoughts like, "You're not from the right family. You don't even have a family. No wonder you can't succeed." Don't believe those lies. Believe this instead: I am who God says I am. I can do what God says I can do.

Too many times, we confuse our performance with our identity. You may have failed, but you're not a failure. Our failures are far more significant than our successes in shaping who we are. God uses it all to shape our testimony. Every disappointment, every wrong, and every closed door has helped make you who you are. Embrace it.

Timing is Everything

Another lesson from reflecting in reverse is that in life, timing is everything. We have to wait for God's timing to get God's best. We must learn the power of contentment over the pursuit of convenience.

Take relationships, for instance. Too often, people get into the wrong relationship and pay for it for the rest of their lives because they can't wait for the right person. "But they that wait upon the Lord shall renew their strength; they shall mount up with wings as eagles; they shall run, and not be weary; and they shall walk, and not faint" (Isaiah 40:31 KJV). When you don't *wait* on God, you will carry *weight*. You have to see things in reverse. Wait for God's best and be thankful for what you have while trusting Him for what you don't have yet. As 1 Thessalonians 5:18 says, "Be thankful in all circumstances, for this is God's will for you who belong to Christ Jesus" (NLT).

While you may receive your calling early in life, your mission may not be revealed for many years. Be good with that! I was 41 when I received my mission. Now, I know what I will do for the rest of my life. My purpose is clear: to bring hope to special needs families. God has a purpose for you, too, even if you don't see it right now.

Live As a Healer

Lastly, if I could see things in reverse, I would tell you to live as a healer. Look for opportunities every day, not to get but to give. Instead of hoping for 20 people to take a sincere interest in you, find two people and take a sincere interest in them. People will care about what matters most to you when you care about what matters most to them.

Looking back on my life, I spent far too much time trying to be affirmed by people rather than using my gifts to affirm others. As you are on your journey, find ways to build and bring healing to others. Romans 12:8 says, "If your gift is to encourage others, be encouraging. If it is giving, give generously. If God has given you leadership ability, take the responsibility seriously. And if you have a gift for showing kindness to others, do it gladly" (NLT).

Have you ever heard someone say, "You didn't have to do that!" By that, they mean, "You did that little extra most people wouldn't do. Thank you!

I recall a story of such a man, who, in 1949, Time Magazine called "one of the most extraordinary men of modern times." He received numerous honors and accolades, including the Nobel Peace Prize. One afternoon, reporters and city officials gathered at a Chicago railroad station to greet him. As passengers disembarked the train, a 6-foot-4-inch giant of a man with a bushy mustache and thick, unruly hair was among them. Cameras flashed! City officials approached him with hands outstretched. The man greeted them politely and then, looking over their heads, asked to be excused for a moment. He quickly walked through the crowd until he reached the side of an elderly woman struggling with two large suitcases. He picked up the bags with a smile and escorted the woman to the bus. After helping her aboard, he wished her a safe journey. He then returned to the greeting party and apologized, "Sorry to have kept you waiting." The man was Dr. Albert Schweitzer, the famous missionary doctor who spent his life helping the poor in Africa. In response to Schweitzer's action, one member of the reception committee said, "That's the first time I ever saw a sermon walking."

Your generosity to someone else may be the most significant message you will ever preach. When you can bear someone's pain without breaking, you will bring them hope and become a healer in their life. You can't control all the struggles from the past, but you can control who holds your future.

God sees everything in reverse. He knows how your story ends. When we see things forward, they look imperfect. When God sees in reverse, they look complete. All the pieces of the puzzle are not yet in your hands. Trust God with your heart. He knows which piece fits today and how to put all the pieces of your life together in the future.

Pray this: Dear God, I can't see past this moment right now, but You see everything from the beginning to the end. You are putting all the pieces of the puzzle together. It's going to be so good. Today, I will lean into Your hope and grace for me. My trust is in You alone. Amen (So be it).

Declare this: Not only will God lead me through any challenges I face, but I trust He will also lead me to victory. Even though I only see things partially, He sees things clearly. I don't have to know all the answers; I just have to believe that God will answer when I call. He will work everything out. I will fulfill my purpose and destiny.

Win for today: I will remind God of every promise He has given me and trust Him to accomplish it.

4
Don't Settle for Baloney

"Why spend your money on food that does not give you strength? Why pay for food that does you no good? Listen to me, and you will eat what is good. You will enjoy the finest food" (Isaiah 55:2 NLT).

We all experience changes and challenges in life. No matter your difficulties, I encourage you to stay faithful, stay the course, and do not settle. The enemy can't stop God's plan for your life, but he'll do his best to convince you to compromise along the way.

If you're going to become all you were created to be, you must keep a fire in your spirit. There has to be a holy determination and resolve that says, "I refuse to settle for less than what God's promised me." You have to make up your mind: you won't be talked out of it. You're not going to water it down. You're not going to let "good enough" be good enough. It may take longer than you thought; it may be more difficult. The good news is that it's not too late. You haven't missed your chance. What God promised you is still on the way. It is not a watered-down version, not a partial healing, not a make-do promotion, and not a good enough marriage, but it is precise*ly* what God promised you. What you were excited about before the delays and bad breaks is still within reach.

God doesn't abort a dream. He doesn't get talked out of what He's promised. He doesn't water down what He's spoken to us. Maybe you're not experiencing this favor because you've settled or accepted that your dreams will not happen. "You'll never get well. Your child will never develop. You'll never get out of debt." If you allow those thoughts to remain, your life will be limited.

It's time to pull up your stakes and pack up your belongings. Mediocrity is not your home. Good enough is not your destiny. Getting by is not where you belong. You may be there now, but that is not your permanent location. Don't settle for an okay marriage, okay job, okay health, or okay life. Yes, we should be content, but we must not settle for anything less than what God put in our hearts.

Sometimes, instead of stirring up our faith and believing for the best, we move the goalposts to justify our compromises. "I can't seem to break this addiction. Managing it will be good enough." "I'll never reach my dreams, but I'm keeping up with my coworker. That's not too bad." No! Instead of justifying our disappointment, leave the goal to God and say, "God, I don't see how this will work out. I don't see how I can get well, how my family will be restored, or how I can reach my dreams. But God, I know You wouldn't make a promise you don't intend to keep. I know You have a way where I don't see a way. I'm not going to settle here. I'm going to keep believing, keep dreaming, and keep stretching my faith". That's the kind of prayer that allows God to do great things.

In Genesis 15, God told Abraham he would have a son. One small problem: Abraham was 75 years old, and his wife, Sarah, was 65. They had never had children, as Sarah had been barren. Now, after she had gone through the change of life, the birth of a child was impossible in the natural. Year after year went by with no sign of a baby. Every thought echoed, "It's been too long. You're wasting your time. You're both too old. It's never going to happen." Finally, in an attempt to have a child, Sarah told Abraham to sleep with her maid. The promise seemed so impossible that she watered it down. She reduced it to the only way she thought it could happen.

Many times, we respond like Sarah. When God speaks to us, instead of raising our faith to His level – believing for the unusual, the uncommon, and the extraordinary – we bring the promise down to our level.

You've got to believe that God can do the impossible. The word "impossible", at first glance, seems quite negative. It's easy to lose hope when you see or hear something that looks impossible. When we lose hope, we open the door to desperation. We allow the winds of doubt to start blowing in our minds. Our initial reaction often includes thoughts like, "This is never going to happen", "It's over", or "What am I going to do?" But how you respond depends on the foundation you're standing on. Are you standing on a foundation of God's word and His promises or are you standing on what you think is impossible. What we build our faith on determines how we are moved. Christ alone is our firm foundation. All self-effort is like quicksand. The harder you try, the deeper you sink.

Matthew 7:26-27 (NIV) says, "But everyone who hears these words of mine and does not put them into practice is like a foolish man who built his house on sand. The rain came down, the streams rose, and the winds blew and beat against that house, and it fell with a great crash."

Imagine two foundations that look similar. One is built on faith, the other is built on fear. One represents standing on sand, and one represents standing on the rock. When you're standing on sand and the doctor says "cancer", you say, "well that's it, maybe my life is over". Sinking sand. When your child gets the diagnosis of autism you fear the worst and lose hope. Sinking sand. You just made a huge mistake, you've hurt people, and you say, "I can't come back from this. It's done." You're standing in sinking sand.

Matthew 7:24-25 (NIV) says, "Therefore everyone who hears these words of mine and puts them into practice is like a wise man who built his house on the rock. The rain came down, the streams rose, and the winds blew and beat against that house; yet it did not fall, because it had its foundation on the rock."

When you're standing on the rock and the doctor says "cancer", but you say, "I will live and not die and declare the works of the Lord, by His stripes I am healed." Firm Foundation. Your child is diagnosed with autism, but you say, "My children are blessed, and they will be mighty in the land." Firm Foundation. You made a huge mistake, but you say, "I may suffer a little while, but God will himself restore, support, strengthen and establish me." Firm Foundation.

I actually love the word "impossible" When you break it down, it says, "I'm possible."

Because what is impossible with man is possible with God. With God "I'm possible!" With God, all things are possible! I Can do all things through Christ who makes it possible! Don't settle where you are, believe for the impossible. Don't settle for what you've always had, believe for what you've never experienced.

Too many of us have accepted our current reality. We have gotten used to just getting by. You should raise your expectations beyond "get by" and good enough. Keep believing for breakthroughs. Keep believing for miracles. Your miracle might not look like someone else's, but that doesn't make it any less of a miracle. Don't lose the sense that God can still do it! He can heal. He can restore. He can do what man can't, but you must stand up and be counted. Declare what is yours!

As a kid, I remember my dad packing the family car for road trips. We inevitably passed a McDonald's or Denny's on every trip, but our family didn't have the money to stop. So, straight past the McDonald's, we drove to find the local minimart grocery store. My dad would buy a loaf of Wonder Bread and a package of bologna for sandwiches. We did this on every single trip. Every.

Single. Trip! It came to the point where I *hated* bologna. At seven years old, I declared from the backseat of the car, "Dad, I'm *never* eating a bologna sandwich again!" My dad thought I was crazy, but I meant it.

And you know what? I have never eaten bologna again! Right after I got home from that trip, I started a job delivering newspapers and saved my money. When we left on our next road trip, I had saved enough money to drive past the grocery store straight to McDonald's! That Big Mac and fries tasted so good!

Sometimes, we settle for bologna when God wants to give us a steak! As a seven-year-old, I made a declaration that I had enough of what I'd always had. Today, I'm asking you to make that same declaration for yourself. Keep praying and believing that God can turn around your situation! Do your best, and let God do the rest. Let's not settle, no matter what comes against us. You are a victor, not a victim. Live like it. No baloney!

Pray this: Dear God, I will not settle. I am Your child, and You want to bless me. I believe my best days are in front of me. Today, I choose to believe that the best is yet to come. Amen (So be it).

Declare this: Today, I choose to do more than just get by. I will move forward believing for God's best. No matter the challenge, I will find what is good about my situation and make it better. I will stand on Your promises and see the goodness of God. I will make today the best day I can, and I will experience the goodness of God.

Win for today: I will set a small goal to finish by the end of the day.

5

A Year To Remember

"Remember not the former things, nor consider the things of old. Behold, I am doing a new thing; now it springs forth, do you not perceive it? I will make a way in the wilderness and rivers in the desert" (Isaiah 43:18–19 ESV).

What if this year became the best year of your life? Not a perfect year or a year without challenges, but a year full of growth and learning. A year where God brings you and your family out and up to a new level. Could you imagine having an unprecedented year? One definition of unprecedented is "Without previous instance; never before known or experienced; unexampled or unparalleled." *A year to remember!*

What if you look back at the end of this year and say, "I remember" or "I will never forget" what God did? Could this year be a memorial stone for you and your family?

What if, right now, you begin to speak this reality over yourself or your situation? Go ahead! Boldly say it out loud:

"I declare that hard things will become easier. I speak restoration in my relationships, healing from loss, and unique opportunities to come my way. This year, I will give more, help more, and fight more for people than I ever have. Favor and blessings will chase me down. Doors that were closed will swing wide open. Hope that was lost will be found. Dreams I had locked away in my heart will break through. I will tell my children and grandchildren what I've witnessed this year. I will celebrate the fact that what should have taken twenty-five years took place in one. *This* will be my year to remember!"

How do you feel after speaking that over your life? Did you feel faith rise? Do you believe it? You might say, "Craig, just because you say it doesn't mean it will happen." You're right. But if you say it and believe God can do it, it can happen.

The Bible says in Mark 11:23, "I tell you the truth, you can say to this mountain, 'May you be lifted up and thrown into the sea,' and it will happen. But you must really believe it will happen and have no doubt in you'" (NLT).

Are you still a doubter? Are you still saying, "I don't believe that." Then this isn't for you at this time. This is for believers. But what if, just maybe, half of what you declared came to pass? Would it be worth it? Why don't you get your faith up, believe again, and see what God can do? You've got nothing to lose and everything to gain. Go for it, and you'll grow for it.

With all that's happening in the world, some people only expect the worst, while God plans the *best*. He's just waiting for you to believe; this will be *a year to remember*!

Pray this: Dear God, I am putting my faith out there. This will be my year to remember. You said if we had the faith of a mustard seed, we could move mountains by Your power. I believe what You say. I am asking You to move mountains in my life today. Amen (So Be It).

Declare this: This year will be a year to remember, a year I will never forget. I will grow and be a blessing to more people than ever. It will be a breakthrough year of God's abundance. I will stand and look back in awe of God and all He orchestrated in my life.

Win for today: Make a short list of a few big dreams in your life. Believe and pray over them today.

6

Speaking With God's Voice (Praying Scripture)

"As the rain and the snow come down from Heaven, and do not return to it without watering the earth and making it bud and flourish, so that it yields seed for the sower and bread for the eater, so is My Word that goes out from my mouth: It will not return to me empty, but will accomplish what I desire and achieve the purpose for which I sent it" (Isaiah 55:10–11 NIV).

Did you know Scripture wasn't just meant to be spoken, but it was meant to be prayed? God is speaking through His words. When you pray Scripture, you are using the most powerful voice in the universe over your life. The Bible says, "The word of God is living and powerful, and sharper than any two-edged sword" (Hebrews 4:12 NKJV). One day, God told me, "I love that you talk to Me when you pray, but begin to speak My words and watch what I will do."

So, we began to practice this, starting with our children. We found promises in God's Word related to each unique child. We circled those Scripture promises and prayed them over each one. Different phases of our children's lives would require different Scriptures. When they needed strength, we prayed Philippians 4:13, which says, "I can do all things through Christ who strengthens me" (NKJV). When they were afraid, we prayed Isaiah 41:13, "For I, the Lord your God will hold your right hand, saying to you, 'Fear not, I will help you'" (NKJV). If they had to take a test in school, we prayed Proverbs 10:7, "The memory of the righteous is blessed" (NKJV).

As each child faced challenges, we found specific Scriptures to pray over them. Cory needed confidence. For him, we prayed Philippians 1:6, "For I am confident of this very thing, that he who began a good work in you will protect it until the day of Christ Jesus" (NASB1995). Courtney had high expectations and felt down if she didn't meet them. We would pray Jeremiah 29:11, "'For I know the plans I have for you,'" declares the Lord, "' plans to prosper you and not to harm you, plans to give you hope and a future'"

(NIV). Connor battled autism, which brought anxiety and meltdowns. We prayed Philippians 4:6-7, "Do not be anxious about anything, but in every situation, by prayer and petition, with thanksgiving, present your requests to God. And the peace of God, which transcends all understanding, will guard your hearts and your minds in Christ Jesus" (NIV).

God did miracles through those prayers. Cory overcame some of his biggest fears. Now, he's a person of faith and a great encourager to others. Courtney kept dreaming big but never got overly discouraged when things didn't work out. Now, she's doing incredible work in the film industry. Connor overcame having meltdowns and is now impacting the world through his inspirational story.

Find Scriptures that speak to the struggles you are carrying. If you are facing financial hardship, find Scriptures on finances and God's provision. If you need healing, search for Scriptures on healing. If you're battling with mental health challenges, find out what God's Word says about worry or anxiety. Let God speak over what you need.

Pray this: Dear God, you said in Your Word that Your promises are yes and amen. As I pray Scriptures, I believe You speak on my behalf. Your voice is powerful. You spoke the world into existence. You spoke and raised Lazarus from the dead. When You speak, miracles happen. I can't wait to see all that You will do by the power of Your Word. Amen (So be it).

Declare this: I will pray God's Word and watch God do what He says He will do. Impossible things will become possible. A shift in the atmosphere is happening in my situation. Dreams that seemed out of reach are within my grasp. I believe God will do it again in my life.

Win for today: Find three scriptures focused on what you're believing God will do and pray those scriptures today.

7
Get Out of the Tent

"The Lord had said to Abram, 'Leave your native country, your relatives, and your father's family, and go to the land that I will show you. I will make you into a great nation. I will bless you and make you famous, and you will be a blessing to others. I will bless those who bless you and curse those who treat you with contempt. All the families on earth will be blessed through you.'" (Genesis 12:1–3 NLT).

Have you ever been camping or taken a trip to the wilderness? You likely set up a tent where you could sleep and stay protected from the elements. But what would the trip be like if you stayed inside the tent the entire time? You would miss out on hiking, fishing, enjoying nature, and all the adventure waiting beyond the tent.

Sometimes, when we face challenges, it's easy to stay in the tent and miss the adventure. We've been hurt, something didn't work out, we're down, and we've lost our passion.

Abram felt that way. He and his wife Sarai couldn't have children. This was so heavy on Abram that he wondered if he would ever have a child or if descendants could come from him. So, he did like many of us do when we are down: he became sad, went in the tent, and agonized over whether his dreams would ever come to pass.

I remember when my wife Sam and I felt that way. We had just gotten the diagnosis that our son had autism, and all the dreams we had for our son seemed unreachable now. We wanted to stay in our tent, so to speak, and shelter ourselves from the pain. Many special needs parents feel this when receiving their diagnosis. They think the vision they had for their child is over. So many stay shut in their homes, sheltering themselves from the world. But sometimes, the things that break your heart also fix your vision.

One day, I read this passage in Genesis 15:5-6: "Then the Lord took Abram outside of his tent and said to him, 'Look up into the sky and count the stars if you can. That's how many descendants you will have!' And Abram believed the Lord, and the Lord counted him righteous because of his faith" (NLT). Because Abram got out of his tent, God did what He promised: Abram's descendants were as many as the stars. We are all spiritual descendants of Abraham. I knew then that if I got out of the tent and looked up at the stars by faith, God would bring our dreams to pass. Sure enough, God pointed us to our destiny.

Not only have our dreams come to pass, but He has exceeded our dreams for our son and allowed us, through our church, to impact thousands of special needs families around the world. We've experienced some of our greatest days outside of the tent.

Maybe you feel like you're in the tent today. You've kept yourself sheltered, worrying that your dreams won't come to pass. You've lost your passion, played it safe, afraid of what may come. *But you can't get your new while holding on to your now.* It's time to believe again! Like Abram, put your faith into action. God has big plans for you. You're a star just waiting to shine. If you do what we did, get out of your tent, and look up at the stars, God will honor your faith and bring your dreams to pass as He did for us.

Pray this: Dear God, I am done staying in isolation. I pray You will help me get out of my tent and look up at the stars as You did for Abraham. You made his descendants as many as the stars in the sky. If you did it for him, I know you can do it for me. Amen (So be it).

Declare this: Today is a new day. I will break old habits and chains that hold me back. I will win the emotional battles that have held me back. I will not look back but look forward to the amazing things God has for me. As I leave my tent and look at the stars, God will bring my hopes and dreams to pass.

Win for today: Go outside your house this evening and look at the stars. Let it remind you of your *big* God and what He can do in your life.

8

From Humble Beginnings to Great Endings

"Do not despise these small beginnings, for the Lord rejoices to see the work begin, to see the plumb line in Zerubbabel's hand" (Zechariah 4:10 NLT).

All of us have a story to tell of where our life began. Some of our beginnings were more fortunate than others, but we all start somewhere. We all have a story.

Maybe you came from humble beginnings. You didn't have the advantages others had, so dreaming big seemed unrealistic. Perhaps you had something great but lost it, and now you feel like you're starting from scratch. But from humble beginnings come great things. It's not where you start; it's where you finish. The struggle is not the end; it's where hope begins.

The challenge is that we spend so much of our lives inside our heads.

You see, we all come with a box. This box is filled with what we know, what we have learned, where we started, and the experiences that have shaped us. If we don't learn to get out of the box, we stop growing and will accept whatever reality our box represents.

But God isn't in our box. He is what we call "outside the box." Out-of-the-box thinking means to think differently, unconventionally, or from a new perspective. That's how Jesus thinks. He thinks *big*, impossible, out-of-the-box thoughts.

You see, God consistently tries to get you out of your box and into His way of thinking. He's just waiting for you to believe what He believes about you. Remember that it's not where you're at but where you are going that matters. But to reach your destiny, you must push back the negative thoughts that keep you in your box.

A recent study says the average brain has 50,000 thoughts. Of those thoughts, 85% are negative. That's over 42,000 thoughts filled with fearful, sad, and discouraging information that fills your mind daily. These thoughts can keep you from what you were designed to do.

I love the story of John Osteen. He grew up in a poor farming family that lost everything during the Great Depression. Things were so bad that their family received Christmas baskets designated for the poorest family in town. John dropped out of high school to help on the farm and got a job selling popcorn in a Fort Worth movie theater. He had no future to speak of, no education, and no money. But something happened, and John began to think outside the box.

At 17 years old, he gave his life to Christ, the first in his family. God put a dream in his heart to become a minister. He believed he would have a church with thousands of people one day. Large churches were unheard of in the 1930s. He told his parents he was going to go out and start ministering. They tried to discourage him and said, "John, all you know how to do is work on the farm. You better stay here. You're going to get out there and fail." They meant well; they were trying to protect him but underestimated the "God idea" in his heart. John Osteen went on to pastor and launch great churches, including the one we are privileged to be a part of today, Lakewood Church. He pastored for 40 years alongside his wife, Dodie. Together, they impacted the world. John wasn't the likely one you'd pick to be successful. He didn't have money, influence, or fame. But God loves to choose people who are underestimated, that nobody sees coming, to do brilliant things.

When the odds are against you, and others tell you it won't work out, it's time to get out of the box. You must know that whatever comes your way, God will direct your steps. Don't despise your days of small beginnings, or you will miss your story about to be told.

Somebody needs to hear this today: Your current situation is not your story. This beginning is not your end. This layover is not your destination. It's not how you go; it's where you land. God sees the end from the beginning and will complete and perfect what He started. Listen, God has it all worked out. Let go of the past, and the past will let go of you. I've heard it said that one day, people who don't believe in you will tell everyone how they met you. God is about to elevate you higher than you could have ever dreamed.

Pray this: Dear God, where I am now is not where I am staying. You can take my situation and turn it around. Thank You for your plans for me, which are for good, not disaster. Your plans for me will bring hope and a great future. I stand on that promise. Amen (So be it).

Declare this: I believe God is turning around my situation. I am moving towards my destiny. I am fulfilling the purpose God has for me and my life. The future is bright and full of promise. My best days are out in front of me!

Win for today: Find a respected relative or friend that you have watched God do great things in their life. Ask them to tell you their story of how it all began.

9
Frequency

"After he has gathered his own flock, he walks ahead of them, and they follow him because they know his voice" (John 10:4 NLT).

It's tough to hear God's voice when we're not on the same frequency. When challenges occur, we tend to get distracted, out of alignment, and out of tune.

It's tough to get in agreement with God. It's like a short-wave radio. Shortwave broadcasts can be transmitted over several thousand miles from one continent to another. You can hear people from thousands of miles away when you are on the right frequency. But with one click to the right or left, all you will hear is static. We are often just one click away from being out of tune with God. The enemy doesn't need you to be way off; he needs you to be one click to the right or one click to the left.

Right now, so many voices are vying for our attention. The enemy is the author of confusion. When facing big challenges, we feel like the enemy is chasing us. It's tough to hear God's voice when you are afraid and fearful of what might come.

Elijah knows this all too well. The Bible tells us in 1 Kings that Elijah had just experienced a phenomenal victory over the prophets of Baal. When Ahab told Jezebel what happened to the false prophets on Mount Carmel, she was furious and vowed to kill Elijah within 24 hours. The prophet Elijah was terrified by Jezebel's threats and became so discouraged that he wanted to die.

If you study the story closely, it's clear that Elijah was completely worn out from pushing himself too hard for too long. Elijah's mind and body were exhausted, and his emotions had fallen apart. He was afraid, depressed, discouraged, and hopeless. Elijah was not on the same frequency. He was out of alignment and out of tune with God. Elijah needed God to save him.

The first thing God told Elijah was to eat and rest. He needed to get in a position of peace to hear God's instruction. Next, God told Elijah to stand on the mountain before the Lord. Suddenly, the Lord passed by, and a great wind swept through, but the Lord wasn't in the wind. After the wind, there was an earthquake, but the Lord was not in the earthquake. After the earthquake, there was a fire, but the Lord was not in the fire. After the fire came a still, small voice. When Elijah heard the voice, he got back into agreement with God. God gave him the plan, and all of Elijah's enemies were put to death.

Maybe the next time you sit with God, you should take 10 minutes to pray and 20 minutes to listen. We must listen and recognize when He is speaking.

A man named Buddy participated in the television show *The Biggest Loser*. Starting the show, Buddy weighed 403 pounds. He spent five months away from his family, losing an incredible 150 pounds. When the contestants' families were finally allowed to visit, Buddy's young son didn't recognize his dad standing across the room from him. Suddenly, Buddy called out to his son, and immediately, the boy recognized his dad's voice and ran to him.

You must spend time listening to God speak so you can recognize your Father's voice. Why? You won't always be able to see, touch, or feel God. You'll only know it's God speaking because you intimately know His voice. Talk to Him, spend time with Him, and listen for Him. The more consistently you spend time with God, the more you will recognize His voice and know when He is speaking. He will guide and direct you to the great plans He has for your future.

Pray this: Dear God, help me to discipline myself to spend time with You so I can hear Your voice. I often don't know what to do and need Your guidance. Lead me into victory as I follow You. Amen (So be it).

Declare this: As I take the steps to spend time with God, He will lead me to victory. The more I hear His voice, the more confident I will become. I won't have to make things happen. He will make things happen for me as I trust in Him.

Win for today: Find a quiet place away from the noise and spend ten minutes listening for God's voice. Even if you don't hear anything, receive the peace you find in that moment.

10
Symphoneo

"I also tell you this: if two of you agree here on earth concerning anything you ask, my Father in Heaven will do it for you" (Matthew 18:19).

Today, there are sounds of heaven invading the earth. When you get into agreement with God, something powerful happens. You are in tune with God.

When an A note is played on an instrument, 440 invisible vibrations move through the air as waves. 440 frequencies per second. When that note gets to your eardrum, your eardrum starts to vibrate 440 times per second. It signals the auditory nerve to communicate with the brain that the note you hear is an A. When your auditory nerve tells your voice it's an A, you have an opportunity to come into agreement. The same is true for our relationship with God.

We can come into agreement with God by putting Jesus first in our lives. That's what Jesus did with His Father. Jesus would go in the morning and pray. Perhaps He was preparing for a big task or working through distress and grief, but He wanted to spend time with the Father to find agreement and support. Second, come into agreement by giving thanks in everything, no matter the circumstance. You will get God's attention when you praise Him, whether in the valley or mountain top. Next, come into agreement by speaking God's word and reading what He says about you. When you know who you are and Whose you are, you inherit His strength. Finally, come into agreement with God through your praise and worship. Praise precedes victory, and God responds to the praises of his people.

Today, there are sounds of heaven invading the earth. The Greek word for "agree" is symphoneo. It means to sound together, to agree or to bargain together, to come into an agreement. It is the Greek word from which the word "symphony" is derived. A symphony orchestra uses a large ensemble of instruments under the direction of a maestro to bring all the players and instruments together, making a beautiful piece of music. One person could not achieve the impact of this piece; it's accomplished only when the master brings all of the instruments together in one accord.

We are God's instruments. When you respond to God, you become an instrument on the earth, created to resonate or resound His glorious voice. Agreement with God causes you to hear His voice, where you can be on the same "key" as God. You are not only hitting the same note, but the sounds from heaven connect with the instruments, you and I, on earth. Now, you have a *symphoneo*. When it all comes together, miracles can happen. God goes into action; heaven invades the earth. Then, God speaks.

Pray this: Dear God, there is nothing more critical in Your Word than coming into agreement with You. Let me be Your instrument here on earth to resound Your voice. I know when we agree, something beautiful happens. Amen (So be it).

Declare this: As I agree with God, something spectacular is about to happen: a big sound invading the earth. My story has yet to be written, but I know God has already designed the soundtrack of my life. I am His masterpiece, and He is doing His greatest work in my life.

Win for today: Spend ten minutes in praise and worship of God today. Give Him thanks for all He has done.

11
Who Told You That

"You are of God, little children, and have overcome them, because He who is in you is greater than he who is in the world" (1 John 4:4 NKJV).

In the Garden of Eden, Adam and Eve lived confidently and securely with God. They knew they had His blessing and favor. But one day, the enemy deceived them into eating the forbidden fruit, and immediately, they were afraid. They ran and hid. When God called out to Adam, "Where are you?" Adam said, "We're hiding because we're naked." The Bible says Adam and Eve knew no shame until the serpent deceived them. God asked, "Who told you that you were naked?" God asked the question, knowing it was the deceiver, but to communicate the shame was not from Him. Some of us are also living with shame that God never put on us.

The enemy loves to whisper who-told-you lies. "You'll never be good enough. Nobody likes you. You're a failure. You're too short or too tall. Nobody wants you. You are too weird and too different. You will never do anything with your life. I wish you were never born. You are not talented. I wish you were more like your brother or sister. You have no potential. You are not smart enough. You're from the wrong family. You never do anything right and will never accomplish your dream." But 1 John 4:4 says, "You are of God, little children, and have overcome them, because He who is in you is greater than he who is in the world" (NKJV).

If you have ever seen a circus act with a lion and its trainer, you might have wondered why the trainer would arm himself with a stool and point its legs toward the beast. The answer is simple: distraction. As powerful as the beast is, distractions can immobilize it. If this man-eater is not distracted occasionally, it might remember what it's capable of and maul the trainer to death! The devil is like the trainer. He knows you have the Lion of Judah and the power of God within you. So, he tries to take your power and immobilize you with who-told-you lies. He wants fear to stop you.

Experts tell us that babies have two natural fears: the fear of falling and loud noises. A study on fear was conducted on 500 adults of varying ages, backgrounds, and lifestyles. The results showed that they shared 7,000 different fears. This means that they must have learned 6,998 fears since they were born. We have absorbed so much fear from bad experiences or other people! When, in actuality, our bodies are designed for faith.

We get afraid when we listen to the wrong voices. Some people have listened to the wrong voice for so long that they no longer remember their true identity. Like the lion, they don't know what they're capable of. They've let the enemy train their minds. They've let people label them, telling them what they're not or can't do. They've allowed circumstances, mistakes, and disappointments to define them. Now, they've lost their passion. If you let other voices continue to rule, they will keep you from your destiny.

Your Creator knows who you really are. He calls you a masterpiece. He said you've been fearfully and wonderfully made.

God asks us today, "Who told you you're not good enough? Who said you're just average or can't accomplish your dreams?" Those negative thoughts didn't come from our God. Don't let the enemy deceive you. You are a child of God.

Sam and I had to do that very thing when our son, Connor, was diagnosed with autism. Doctors told us what Connor would never be or do. They said he would never speak, graduate from high school, get a job, or live outside the home. But God reminded us of who Connor was created to be. Everything we were told was impossible has happened. Connor not only speaks, but his first words were the full "This Is My Bible" declaration we say at Lakewood. He graduated from high school, got a job at Whataburger, and now lives with other roommates outside of the home.

You have to believe what God says about you. Many people are more influenced by what others say they should be instead of who God says they are. Someone will tell you what you should be if you don't know who you are. Today, know that God sees your potential. He knows what you're capable of. You may feel weak, but God calls you strong. You may be intimidated, but God calls you confident. You may feel less than, but God calls you well-able. Get in sync with God and start believing what He says about you!

Pray this: Dear God, I believe in what you say about me. You have great plans for me. I will tune out other voices and know I am a child of God made in Your image. My future is bright because You are fighting for me. Amen (So be it).

Declare This: I am a child of God and will believe what God has declared over my life. I will avoid negative voices and trust in the one voice that matters. God says I am blessed, and I cannot be cursed. God says I am the head and never the tail. God says I can do all things through Christ who strengthens me.

Win for today: Write three positive things God says about you in His Word on a sticky note. Then, place it on your mirror or refrigerator and remind yourself who God says you are throughout the day.

12
God Will Rescue You

"Before they call I will answer; while they are yet speaking I will hear" (Isaiah 65:24 ESV).

Have you ever wondered what the letters SOS stand for? Many think it's an abbreviation for "save our souls" or "save our ship," but those phrases are backronyms. When wireless radio telegraph machines first made their way onto ships around the turn of the 20th century, sailors in danger needed a way to attract attention, signal distress, and ask for help. They needed a unique signal to be transmitted clearly and quickly, indicating they needed to be rescued.

We all have times when we need to send an SOS, asking God to save us from our distress and come to the rescue. Maybe today, you need to be rescued from a circumstance. The faster you signal for rescue, the faster you can escape that situation. God often sends people, ministries, or humanitarian organizations to help others, giving them what they need when they need it most. I've heard it said that God uses rescued people to rescue people. God is constantly listening for our calls for help. He knows us intimately and knows what we need before we ever ask. That's how proactive and attentive our God is to your SOS.

I have heard many amazing stories of people being rescued, like my friend Nate. Nate had been homeless most of his adult life and was carrying hurts and pains from his childhood. One day, Nate was sitting at a metro bus stop, and a lady from our church invited him to Lakewood. Nate said yes. He came to church and accepted Jesus. Shortly after, a man named John Bowman began to walk alongside Nate. He helped him get a job and attend classes at church, where he started to work through his anger issues and feelings of abandonment. Nate continued to work through ups and downs for two years while mostly living on the street. But John and the men of our church never gave up on him.

In 2017, after Nate's childhood home flooded during Hurricane Harvey, his mom gave Nate the deed. Unfortunately, the house was unlivable. The men of our church helped rebuild the flooded home. After a year of work and mostly volunteer labor, Nate was no longer homeless. God rescued Nate! In 2019, John married Nate and his new bride, Courtney. Nate now owns his own business, and he and Courtney are about to welcome their second child.

Another story comes from my friend Angel and her mentor, Shannon Nelson. From the time Angel was a little girl, she has experienced more pain than one person should. She is what we would call the ultimate "survivor." Despite the abuse, drugs, and pain, she kept fighting. Angel fought for herself, but she mainly fought for her four kids. At her lowest moment, Angel was forced into sex trafficking and thought about giving up on life. But she remembered a verse in Deuteronomy 30:19 that said, "This day I call the heavens and the earth as witnesses against you that I have set before you life and death, blessings and curses. Now choose life, so that you and your children may live" (NIV). God heard her SOS and gave her the courage to run away. She found two of our church members, Sean and Shannon Nelson, who lead the Dream Center in the Houston area. Since then, her life has completely turned around. Angel is now an intern at the Dream Center and brings girls going through similar situations to church. She's sober and drug-free. She's been reunited with her four children and is now a member of our church.

More personally, my family has its own story of God's rescue. In the late 1940s, my dad's family lived in California, picking fruit as field workers in orchards and living in a little shanty down by the Stanislaus River. My grandfather, drinking with friends after work, waded into the river to swim. The current swept him away, and my grandfather drowned, leaving my grandmother with three young boys and no money to speak of. A pastor from 5th and G Tabernacle in Fresno, California, read my family's plight in the newspaper. He brought groceries to their little home and invited them to church. That pastor mentored my dad, who eventually became a pastor. I'm standing here today because God used that pastor to rescue my family.

What do you need rescuing from today? Your circumstance may not be as intense as these stories, but whatever it is, God is in the rescuing business. Send out your SOS today and watch the greatest Hero of all come to your rescue. God wants to heal you, restore you, provide for you, and bring your ruins back to life.

Pray this: Dear God, You know what I need before I even ask for it. So, I'm sending out my SOS today. Please make a way where there seems to be no way. Come to my rescue. Amen (So be it).

Declare this: Lord, I believe You are coming to my rescue today. I don't have to worry or be afraid. My Hero is on His way. You are about to show up in my situation and turn it around. What was lost will be found. Not only will You rescue me, but You will use my situation to catapult me into my destiny.

Win for today: Write down where you need God's rescue. It may not even be for you but for someone else. Leave a space below what you've written. Keep it in a safe place, and pray over it today. When God comes through, write down what He did to rescue the situation. Share that testimony to encourage others.

13

Coming Out of the Drought

"I prayed to the Lord, and He answered me. He freed me from all my fears" (Psalm 34:4 NLT).

Sometimes, life doesn't go as planned. You think you walked through the right door, but life seemingly takes a wrong turn. You find yourself in the desert, a drought of epic proportions with adversity on every side.

Psalm 84:5-7 (NKJV) is one of my favorite Scriptures when facing a desert season.

Verse 5 starts, "Blessed is the man whose strength is in You." You are not in the desert to die. You are in the desert for God to show you a new way to live. God is getting you ready for something bigger. If you don't go through this time of testing, you won't be able to handle what God is about to give you. Trust Him. He's going to take you places you've never been.

The Scripture continues in verse 5, "Whose heart is set on pilgrimage." Some droughts are short; some can be longer. But here's the key: don't give up! Keep going. You can only fail if you stop moving forward. You only have grace for today. So take one day at a time, and make today the best you can.

Verse 6 continues, "As they pass through the Valley of Baca." The Valley of Baca, which this Scripture speaks of, was part of the desert country. It was filled with thorns, wild animals, vipers, and all sorts of danger. It was nearly impossible to travel through this valley without suffering extreme hardship. Yet this valley was the only passageway into the high hills where Israel's Cities of Refuge was located. Some scholars state the Valley of Baca also represented the valley that led to Jerusalem, where the temple of God was found.

When we're experiencing a drought, we can do three things. First, we can look down. Of course, that's not good because we can only see the ground. Second, we can look straight ahead. That's better, but the human eye can only see so far. Or, we can look up. When we look up, God will see what we could never see. He sees the victory ahead and will give us faith to keep walking until we arrive.

The Scripture goes on to say, "They make it a spring; The rain also covers it with pools. They go from strength to strength." You see, once you've conquered the desert you're in, you won't respond to the next desert the same way. You move from a survivor to an overcomer. Your test becomes your testimony. You live in the vision and not in the circumstance.

Some of you are facing difficult struggles right now. Maybe you've forgotten what rain feels like. You have been in droughts in your relationships, battling with sickness, or the death of a loved one. Your children are struggling; you're facing financial issues or the loss of a job. You have been faced with overwhelming obstacles for months or even years.

When you're in a drought or facing adversity, there is something that can bring you out of the drought and into an abundance of rain. Pray bold prayers! Don't just pray "get by" prayers of desperation. The Bible says to come boldly to the throne of grace. Make your petitions known to God. Psalm 22:5 says, "They cried out to you and were saved. They trusted in you and were never disgraced" (NLT).

Droughts are not the time to complain; they are the time to proclaim.

There is no power in complaining. Complaining is the language of the disempowered.

When God was bringing the children of Israel out of Egypt and into the promised land, the trip was only supposed to take 11 days. But the children of Israel began to complain and murmur, and what was only supposed to be an 11-day journey took 40 years.

When we face things initially, we might need to release feelings to get them off our chest. But let me encourage you not to stay in the land of complaining and murmuring. Like the children of Israel, it will take you nowhere. Begin to pray bold prayers. Begin to believe God can do it. Every day, when you wake up, start with a bold prayer. Declare truth over your situation. God responds to bold prayers.

You may be in a drought today. You may have forgotten what the abundance of rain feels like, but a shift is about to happen. You will not only come out of your drought; you will go from strength to strength. You will come out better than you were before.

Pray this: Dear God, I come boldly to your throne of grace. I believe you are making a way through the desert today. I will pray big and believe big because you are a big God. Amen (So be it).

Declare this: I am coming out of the drought and into the abundance of rain. I will not struggle as I have before. I will pray boldly and watch God end my drought. I am more than a conqueror. My test will become my testimony. I will live in the vision and not the circumstance. I am no longer a survivor; I am an overcomer!

Win for today: Pray a bold prayer over your circumstance today.

14

The God of The Comeback

"For though the righteous fall seven times, they rise again" (Proverbs 24:16 NIV).

Everyone loves a comeback story, don't they? No one remembers the blowouts in games, but everyone remembers a comeback. It's impossible to forget a moment you're down and out, but fight to come back.

You may know baseball player Trey Mancini by name, but you've likely never heard his whole story. Outside of being a great baseball player, in 2020, Trey was diagnosed with stage 3 colon cancer and faced tremendous odds against him. He underwent surgery and chemotherapy and, most importantly, trusted God. Trey returned to play in the big leagues a year later and earned American League Comeback Player of the Year. A 2021 campaign during which he re-established himself as one of the game's best hitters after a year away battling and beating stage 3 colon cancer.

Beyond comeback stories in sports, we're inspired to hear about folks who endured physical, emotional, or financial setbacks but refused to quit. We love to hear stories of those who persevered despite the near-impossible odds they faced.

Did you know that the Bible is full of comeback stories? Take Joseph, for example. His own brothers were jealous of him and sold Joseph into slavery as a young man for 20 pieces of silver. He was rejected by his own family and later thrown into prison for a crime he didn't commit. Yet, Joseph kept doing the right thing, and God turned his life into a comeback story. Joseph eventually became Pharoah's second in command, forgave his brothers, and saw his family restored.

How about Job? He loses his wealth, land, and even his own family. Yet, he never curses God. Job held on through the storms of his life. God rewarded Job for his commitment to Him and blessed him with double what he had before.

And, of course, the most remarkable comeback story of them all: Jesus. Jesus was crucified, dead, and buried, but three days later came back to life and saved the world.

You might say, Craig, you don't know what I've been through. Look, I get it; life can be challenging. When God closes one door, He opens another, but it can be hell in the hallway.

Life is full of things trying to push us down. We all face disappointments and setbacks. Maybe you received some bad news about your health, or perhaps a relationship didn't work out. You've made some mistakes that are difficult to bounce back from. That was a setback. It's easy to get discouraged, lose enthusiasm, or even be tempted to give up.

But, if we're going to see the God of the comeback rewrite our story, we have to have a "comeback" mentality. When you get knocked down, you don't stay down. You dust yourself off and get back up. Know that every time adversity comes against you, the God of the comeback is waiting to step into the ring and deliver the knockout blow to the enemy. We must only not give up and allow God to fight for us.

My friend Prasad, whom I met in Sri Lanka, had to do this. His father had a history of mental health issues. At six years old, Prasad watched his mom go through physical and verbal abuse. The endless fighting, no money, and watching his dad go in and out of hospitals was overwhelming. The abuse continued through Prasad's teenage years until, ultimately, Prasad tried to take his own life. Prasad said, "It was at the lowest point in my life, where anyone couldn't feel more helpless or hopeless, that I experienced the life-transforming power of Jesus, which changed the course of my life." Today, Prasad holds no bitterness towards his dad. He has a beautiful wife and son. He leads the compassion ministry at a church in Sri Lanka, which helps hundreds of thousands of broken families and children with PTSD. He's rewriting his story.

I've heard it said that *sometimes you have to get knocked down lower than you have ever been to stand up taller than you ever were.* Don't let your gifts and anointing end with you. You are facing a challenge; you are not facing defeat. Remember that. Sometimes, rejection is redirection. God is in the business of giving people fresh starts. He is the God of the comeback.

No matter what you left, all that matters now is where you go from here.

God has already arranged a comeback for every setback, a vindication for every wrong, and a new beginning for every disappointment. *The comeback is always greater than the setback.*

As a believer in Jesus, the same power that raised Christ from the dead lives inside you. Your comeback story is about to be written. There is no challenge that is too difficult, no obstacle too large for God. No sickness, no disappointment, no person—nothing can keep you from the purpose God designed just for you. If you stay in faith, God will turn what was meant to harm you and catapult you into your God-given destiny.

Pray this: Dear God, Your Word says though the righteous fall seven times, they rise again. I know You are rewriting my story. You are the God who will help me make a comeback to all I was created to be. Amen (So be it).

Declare this: I know that God is writing my comeback story. It will be better than I ever dreamed. No disappointments or setbacks will keep me from God's plans. My new life is just beginning.

Win for today: Watch or read about an amazing comeback story and let it inspire you today.

15

Make Today the Very Best Day of Your Life

"This is the day that the Lord has made; let us rejoice and be glad in it" (Psalm 118:24 ESV).

What if you got up every day and said, "I'm going to make today the very best day of my life!" That's what a very successful restauranteur named Randy would say when anyone asked how he was doing. At first, people would be taken aback by it, wondering if he was serious. His positive outlook seemed fake or inauthentic to others, but for Randy, it was real. Even if he didn't feel it, he practiced saying it. Then he started believing it, leading him to live it out. It was contagious. Randy always set the tone.

Will Guidara, author of *Unreasonable Hospitality*, says, "Let your energy impact the people you're talking to, as opposed to the other way around."

When Pastor Joel Osteen gets up every morning, the first thing that comes out of his mouth as he jumps out of bed is, "It's going to be a great day." What is he doing? He's setting the tone for his day rather than letting the enemy or someone else set it for him.

Looking at today's Scripture, we see David setting the tone in Psalm 118. He sets the tone by acknowledging who will have control over his day. When you wake up in the morning, who is setting the tone? Your family, the TV, a situation, your phone? Or is it you and God?

I read how the author John Maxwell's friend approached every day. His friend calculated that if the average person lives for 75 years, multiplied by 52 weeks in a year, they will have 3,900 Saturdays in their lifetime. He said, "It took me until I was 55 years old to think about all this in any detail, and by that time, I had lived through over 2,800 Saturdays. I got to thinking that if I lived to be 75, I only had about a thousand of them left to enjoy." He went on to explain that he bought 1,000 marbles and put them in a clear plastic container in his favorite work area at home. "Every Saturday since then," he said, "I have taken one marble out and thrown it away. I found that by watching the marbles diminish, I focused more on the really important things in life. There's nothing like watching your time here on this earth run out to help get your priorities straight." Then the gentleman finished, "Now let me tell you one last thought before I sign off and take my lovely wife out to breakfast. This morning, I took the very last marble out of the container. I figure if I make it to next Saturday, I have been given a little extra time."

Maybe we can't choose how much time we get, but we can determine what we will do with it. Let's set the tone for today and make this day *the very best day of our lives.*

Pray this: Dear God, like David, I want to set the tone for my day. This is the day the Lord has made; I will rejoice and be glad in it. I pray that You will help me make every day the very best day of my life. Amen (So be it).

Declare this: I will try to make today the very best day of my life. I will focus on God and what He can do. Every day, I will make God a priority and allow Him to make it happen. It's going to be a great day! I receive it by faith. I am setting the tone for my day and my future!

Win for today: Start the day by saying, "It's going to be a great day!" Then, throughout the day, when people ask you how you are doing, say, "I'm just trying to make today the very best day of my life." See how it changes your day.

16

Invisible But Invaluable

"So that your giving may be in secret. Then your Father, who sees what is done in secret, will reward you" (Matthew 6:4 NIV).

A few years back, I heard a story about Joel Osteen talking to an equipment manager for a professional basketball team. When the team arrives in the middle of the night, the equipment manager has to go to the arena at 2:00 am to set up. He carefully studies what each player likes and sets up their lockers accordingly. He is so dedicated, but many never see his work. He powerfully said, "I'm invisible, but I'm invaluable. Nobody sees me, but I know I matter. I'm secure enough in who I am that I can be comfortable working behind the scenes. I'm content to make others look good." Wow! He is completely secure, knowing who he is and the value he brings to the team.

We often do our best to make things happen, but nobody sees our effort. It's easy to get discouraged, give up, or stop trying because you don't think anyone cares. But there is someone who does care: God. You could become the focus of His attention when you focus your attention on others. But you must have the attitude that you're sowing a seed and pushing people up, not looking for credit.

I've discovered that when it's your time to shine, God will make sure someone is there to push you up. But you must pass the test of being invisible. I've heard it said like this: If you aren't secure enough to be invisible, you will struggle to feel valuable. In fact, your most important time to serve or give may never be on a stage or platform.

Some may think that the times I stand on a platform or speak to large crowds are my most significant times of influence. Don't get me wrong; it's an important responsibility, and God honors whatever we do for the Lord. But, based on Matthew 6:4, our most impactful work is not on a stage or platform. Our most valuable times of giving may only be seen by a few people. Like serving in kids' ministry as a helper, setting up or tearing down after an event, handing out food to those who are homeless, or encouraging a special needs mom who's had a bad week. There is no fanfare or applause from people, just faithfully doing it unto the Lord.

I know that when I speak in front of a large crowd, many people are behind the scenes making it happen. Their names are not on the sign outside, and their faces aren't on the big screen. Yet the event would not have happened without them. Their names are not written in the program but flashing brightly in heaven. How heaven sees things is different from how we see things. You don't need a title to have influence.

You may not realize that when you do things in secret, without the applause of people, your Father in heaven sees you. Heaven stands at attention when no one else is watching, offering a standing ovation. God says: *Look at my child doing it all for me. I'm so proud of them. Let me reward that. Let me bless them. Let me take them to places they never dreamed of.* What is done in secret, God will reward openly.

Matthew 10:42 says, "And whoever gives to one of these little ones [in rank or influence] even a cup of cold water because he is My disciple, surely, I declare to you, he shall not lose his reward" (AMPC).

You have to learn to be okay with being invisible. Just remember, you're invaluable to the Kingdom.

Pastor Joel says, "True greatness is not how bright you shine but how bright you make others shine." When you build people, God will build you. When you focus on others, you'll have what you need to handle what life brings. You won't let success go to your head, or failure go to your heart.

You can be content in any season when you're secure in who God made you. Learn to be content where you are on the way to where you are going. You don't have to promote yourself. Keep honoring God. When it's your time to be promoted, God will do it.

We read in 1 and 2 Kings about the relationship between Elijah and Elisha. Elisha spent time taking care of Elijah, who was content being invisible. At one point, Elijah wanted to leave Elisha and go away, but Elisha knew his destiny was tied to him. He would not let Elijah go without him. After years of being invisible, Elijah was to be taken to heaven. Elisha had been faithful all those years. Then, when it was his time, Elisha took over and performed twice as many miracles as Elijah.

What am I saying? Be content to play your role. Be okay with being invisible. God may be getting you ready to have more influence. Like Elisha,

He's preparing you to do twice as much of what you've done before. But you have to pass the test of being invisible to receive the blessing of being invaluable.

Pray this: Dear God, I understand now that what is done in secret, You will reward openly. No matter my status in life, I will be secure in who I am on the way to where I am going. Thank you for the privilege of being invisible so I can be valuable to You. Amen (So be it).

Declare this: I am okay with being invisible, knowing God will promote me at the right time. Through my service to others, new doors of opportunity will open. I don't have to be promoted by people. The best promotions come from God. All I have to do is chase after Him, and He will chase after me.

Win for today: Think about what you do for people and God that nobody sees. Thank God for those opportunities.

17

It's Not How You Start, It's How You Finish

"Therefore, since we are surrounded by such a great cloud of witnesses, let us throw off everything that hinders and the sin that so easily entangles. And let us run with perseverance the race marked out for us" (Hebrews 12:1 NIV).

In life, we will all have a start, a middle, and a finish. Some start well; others are less fortunate. But it's not how you start that matters the most; it's how you finish. As we go through life, we get excited at the beginning of an opportunity, a relationship, or a new venture. We also enjoy celebrating our achievements and having the satisfaction of fulfilled desires. But between the beginning and the end, every situation or pursuit has a "middle." The middle is where we often face our greatest challenges, hurdles, roadblocks, and detours.

All of us will face tests. It's inevitable. But it's how you respond to the tests that make the difference.

Many of us witnessed Demar Hamlin of the Buffalo Bills face a test on live TV in front of the world. After making a tackle on the field, Damar suddenly collapsed. Many people, including doctors, wondered if he would ever recover after being carted off. Then something extraordinary happened. Players and coaches began kneeling, lifting their fallen brother up to God. The crowd started praying. Announcers on TV broadcasts began praying for healing. Spectators around the world came together in unity, praying for a miracle. Over the next few days, as the world watched, we saw God do the miraculous. Demar came back to life. When Demar woke up, he asked, "Who won the game?" Doctor Timothy Pitts said, "You've won the game, Damar… the game of life."

You see, for Demar, this injury was a roadblock. It wasn't the end. God is still writing Damar's story. Why? Because he kept running the race even in the face of incredible obstacles. He not only pushed through his near-death experience but, against all odds, returned and played for the Buffalo Bills.

Because he pushed through the "middle," God used his story to change the world.

The enemy wants you to stop short of receiving and enjoying everything God has for you. He will tempt you to give up by making the middle of your journey seem too long or too hard. God, on the other hand, wants the very best for you. Because of the purpose He has for you, God wants you to finish the race set before you.

2 Corinthians 12:9 says, "As you live in close contact with me, the light of my presence filters through you to bless others. Your weakness and woundedness are the openings through which the light of the knowledge of my glory shines forth. My strength and power show themselves most effective in your weakness" (AMP).

Determine to be faithful throughout each part of your story and enjoy your journey to victory. The best way out is always through. It's not how you start that's most important; it's how you finish. You can't go back and change the beginning, but you can start where you are and change the ending.

Pray this: Dear God, with Your help, I will not give up. I will push through the middle and accomplish my dreams. I will run my race with perseverance and finish with joy. Amen (So be it).

Declare This: God sees my potential. He knows what I am capable of. I may feel weak, but God calls me strong. I may be intimidated, but God calls me confident. I may feel less than, but God calls me well-able. I will finish the race God has for my life and push through to victory!

Win for today: Find a friend you admire that you have noticed finishes well. Ask them to share their story and any advice they would give to you.

18

This is How I Fight My Battles

"You will not have to fight this battle. Take up your positions; stand firm and see the deliverance the Lord will give you, Judah, and Jerusalem. Do not be afraid; do not be discouraged. Go out to face them tomorrow, and the Lord will be with you" (2 Chronicles 20:17 NLT).

Having faith doesn't exempt us from difficulties in life. The storms of life come to every person. We get a bad medical report. Our child is not progressing. Our marriage is struggling. In difficult times, it's easy to think, "God, where are You? How could You let this happen to me?" Remember, the God who fights your battles in the good times is the same God who fights your battles in the hard times. God will not allow a difficulty unless He has a divine purpose for it. He never said He would prevent every difficulty, but God did promise to bring you through it and use every difficulty for good.

In my experience, it works best to release control and allow God to fight for us. I've found that peace and control do not go together. When we try to control things, there is no peace. We have to let go of control and receive God's peace. Your lowest points may be launching pads to God's greatest miracles. Don't stress over anything you can't change. Don't use your energy to worry; use your energy to believe.

That's what King Jehoshaphat and the nation of Israel had to do. In 2 Chronicles 20, three armies were going to attack Israel. King Jehoshaphat knew that these three armies would wipe them out. They were too strong and powerful. Have you ever felt like a circumstance would wipe you out? This is how the entire nation of Israel felt. In the natural, they didn't have a chance to win against these armies. But all of a sudden, a man in the middle of the crowd speaks out and says, "This is what the Lord says to you: 'Do not be afraid or discouraged because of this vast army. For the battle is not yours, but God's." (2 Chronicles 20:15 NIV).

The man continued speaking, giving instructions from God to the Israelites. They were told to go to the place of the battle, but instead of fighting, they were to stand firm, give praise to God, and watch God give them victory.

In the natural, that sounds crazy. How can you win a battle without getting in the fight? But that's exactly what they did. It was amazing! One army started fighting another and then another until all three armies were wiped out. Get this: King Jehoshaphat didn't have to lift a finger. He just watched God fight for him. The Bible says not only did they win the battle, but they took back more plunder than they could contain. If you believe, God will fight your battle *and* give you more than you can contain.

Remember: the victory didn't happen until they were willing to let go of control and let God fight for them.

How many of you are fighting battles that God was meant to fight? You've gotten a scary diagnosis or heard some difficult news. Instead of releasing control, you've tried to figure out how to deal with the situation. You've let worry, fear, and the unknown affect you, and now you feel defeated. Can I encourage you to do what King Jehoshaphat did? There comes a point when you've done everything you can: you believed and stood in faith. Now you've got to do what they did: quit fighting. Quit trying to make it happen your way. Quit trying to force it to work out and relinquish control. Let God fight your battle.

Pray this: Dear God, I will do what Jehoshaphat did and let You fight my battle. I am releasing control and trusting you to lead me to victory. Amen (So be it).

Declare this: I know God will fight my battles for me. I will stand firm, believe in faith, and watch God do it. I will stop fighting battles God was meant to fight. The battle is over already. We are victorious. I believe it and declare it!

Win for today: Read 2 Chronicles 20:1-29 and get this story deep inside your spirit. At the end of the reading, declare, "If God did it for Jehoshaphat, God will do it for me!"

19

The Past Is The Past, You Were Made for Something Greater

"So Elijah went from there and found Elisha son of Shaphat. He was plowing with twelve yoke of oxen, and he himself was driving the twelfth pair. Elijah went up to him and threw his cloak around him. Elisha then left his oxen and ran after Elijah. 'Let me kiss my father and mother goodbye,' he said, 'and then I will come with you.' 'Go back,' Elijah replied. 'What have I done to you?' So Elisha left him and went back. He took his yoke of oxen and slaughtered them. He burned the plowing equipment to cook the meat and gave it to the people, and they ate. Then he set out to follow Elijah and became his servant" (1 Kings 19:19–21 NIV).

When God called Elisha to become Elijah's successor, he first burned his plows. Continuing his old trade would keep him from his destiny. What got you here will not get you there. Elisha knew it was God's calling, so he responded. He was not job hunting and was doing pretty well by living standards. I doubt Elisha had any thought that before the day ended, he would leave what he knew so well. A new calling was probably nowhere on his radar when the day began.

God has an unmistakable way of issuing His call. Remember not to seek things that can only be added. Be faithful to God where you are; in due time, He will add what you need.

While Elisha was plowing in complete anonymity, Elijah, the greatest prophet in the Hebrew scriptures, was told to go and anoint him as his successor! I want to encourage you today. Just like God spoke to Elijah, He will speak your name thousands of miles away, at the right time, to the right person.

God was calling Elisha into something different. Are you holding on to old plows when God wants to give you a new purpose?

So, Elisha receives the call and has a choice to make. Will I stay a successful farmer in the family business, or will I follow God's call on my life? The choice was between the family business or a greater calling. Of course, in life, nothing good ever comes easily. The greater calling will cost you something. The cost may be giving up a comfortable, easy life. Elisha chose the more difficult road rather than playing it safe.

I'd rather look back at my life and say, "I can't believe I did that!" instead of, "I wish I did that!" Don't let your gifts and anointing end with you.

I don't know if Elisha had any second thoughts about going with Elijah, burning the plows, or asking for a double portion. But I imagine he regretted nothing when doing double the number of miracles. And you won't either. At least not when you've followed your greater purpose with God and left behind your less-than-desirable life.

What God has in store for you is more significant than you can imagine. You're about to enter a season that will change your life forever for the good. It's time to stop looking back and start moving forward. God is propelling your destiny into place. If you start having second thoughts about a new adventure with God, consider what you will miss: new levels of favor, abundance, and freedom. It's time to burn the plow and experience the rewards of obedience, discovering what the "greater" life looks like.

There has to come a time when we say, "We're all in." It's time! Burn the plows. You were made for something greater!

Pray this: Dear God, when You call, help me to obey and be willing to go all in. I know it's for a greater purpose, and I want to live my life pleasing you. As I do this, I know You will do something greater. Amen (So be it).

Declare this: I believe and declare that I will obey what God asks me to do and follow His will for my life. I know it will be for something greater than I could accomplish alone. New levels of favor and abundance are headed my way. This is my time. This is my moment!

Win for Today: Find a story in the Bible where someone obeyed God and stepped out in faith. Watch how their life changed forever. Let it inspire you!

20

The Gift of Generosity

"Give, and it will be given to you. A good measure, pressed down, shaken together, and running over, will be poured into your lap. For with the measure you use, it will be measured to you" (Luke 6:38 NIV).

During the Christmas season, many children focus on Santa Claus. Although the real reason to celebrate Christmas is Jesus' birth, you may be surprised to hear the true story of Saint Nicholas. You may have thought Santa Claus was a fictional character epitomized by jolly ho-ho-hos, but old Saint Nick was, in fact, a real person, immortalized by his good deeds long after his difficult life on earth ended.

Born wealthy in third-century Greece, Nicholas was orphaned as a small child during a horrific epidemic. In keeping with his Christian teachings, this small, forlorn boy found strength and inner peace by giving away his entire inheritance to those less fortunate than himself. Nicholas later became a bishop, well known for his generous spirit and the delight he found in children. He spent much of his life without material possessions, but his legacy of giving, kindness, and simple joy has outlived him for centuries. He became someone else's miracle through his generosity.

It's easy to go through life focused on ourselves, our dreams, and our challenges, but I've learned that if you become someone else's miracle, God will always take care of you. You can be the answer to someone's prayer. God has no arms to hug except your arms, no voice to encourage except your voice, and no legs to do good deeds except your legs. The heart does the giving; the fingers only let go.

God will put people in our path so we can become the answer to their prayer. You may not realize it, but you're a miracle waiting to happen. Somebody you know will be lonely this holiday season. They're praying for a friend. You can be the miracle they're waiting for.

A video recently went viral showing a young adult displaying a random act of kindness to a 100-year-old veteran. Isaiah Garza is seen approaching an elderly man with a walker, asking him if he wants to go to Disneyland.

The 100-year-old veteran is caught by surprise. "You'd really take me?"

Isaiah explained, "First, we went on the teacups, and it was his first ride in 50 years. Then, [we rode] It's a Small World and sang it together like 50 times. We became best friends for the day."

As the video ends, Isaiah asks the centenarian how it feels to be in the "happiest place on earth." Choking back tears, he says, "This is one of the best days of my life. I thought my life was over. You don't know how much I appreciate this. I will remember this."

Love and giving go hand-in-hand.

When you give your all, it will feel like it costs you nothing. In a society where others are consumed with *accumulating* and *taking*, followers of Jesus should be known as *givers*. We are never more like God than when we give. The closest thing to God's heart is giving to those in need.

Another viral video showed Carlos Davis and his brother, who spotted a woman paying for her gas in pennies. They decided to step in and offer her money to cover the expenses. They didn't realize how much of an impact this act of kindness would have on the woman.

After Davis stepped out of his car to hand the woman the money for gas, she burst into tears and told him that her husband had died just a week prior.

"How did you know?" the woman asked, to which Davis responded, "It's only right, we've got to stick together."

I believe God strategically places people in our lives *every day* to allow us to be the hands and feet of Jesus. It may be your co-worker down the hall at work, someone you see at church, one of our neighbors, or the child with no friends.

When Ashlee Buratti threw a birthday party for her son Glenn, a six-year-old with autism and epilepsy, not one of his 16 classmates showed up. Buratti took to Facebook to describe how heartbroken she felt as the youngster kept asking, "When will my friends come?" "To see the look on his face killed me inside," she wrote.

The local Florida community where she lived quickly rallied to the cause. Burrati was overwhelmed with requests from parents asking if they could come to the birthday party with their children. About 15 children and 25 adults came to eat cake and bring gifts, including a bicycle. The local police and fire department crews also made an appearance, inviting the birthday boy to check out the big red fire engine and take a ride on a police motorcycle.

Listen, you never know what someone else may be going through. Our kindness may compensate for someone else's unkindness.

In the Bible, God said something interesting to Moses when Moses felt he had nothing to give. In Exodus 4:2 (NIRV), God asked Moses, "What do you have in your hand?" In other words, what do you have that's available to you?

Moses answered: All I have in my hand; all I have available is a *shepherd's staff*—a *simple*, *insignificant*, *ordinary* piece of wood.

God said, "Throw it on the ground!" Let Me *use* what's in your hand!

When Moses let go of that staff, releasing it from his hands to give it away, *it was never the same again.*

If you study the Scriptures—that simple, ordinary, insignificant piece of wood—was never called the staff of Moses again. It was called the *Staff of God*! God used that simple shepherd's staff to do incredible things.

Just like Moses, when we *give* what we have in our hands to those in need, God transforms what we release.

Let me encourage you that *every person has something to give!* Every person has God-given gifts, talents, resources, and time to offer. We all have something in our hands!

Pray this: Dear God, I want to be used by You like never before. I pray You will give me discernment to see the needs of others and how I may help them. I'm ready to be used. Amen (So be it).

Declare this: I will give more, help more, and fight for people more this year than ever before. I am a difference maker. As I bless others, God will bless me!

Win for today: Find one person you know who is in need and look for a way to bless them.

21
Faith vs. Fear

"For God has not given us a spirit of fear; but of power, of love, and a sound mind" (2 Timothy 1:7 NKJV).

I heard someone say recently that faith and fear have something in common. They both ask us to believe something we cannot see. I have learned that the more we stay in the moment, the more we can believe. We only have grace for today, so if we can let go of the past, trust God for today, and believe God will take care of our tomorrow, we can win the battle of faith over fear.

What we meditate on will take root. In the Bible, Job said, "The thing I greatly feared has come upon me" (Job 3:25 NKJV). When you are going through a difficult time, learning to have short-term memory and let it go keeps you in a position to trust God. Then, as you turn to God, meditate on what He has done for you and begin to thank Him for what's right, not wrong, in your life. My wife and I have had to practice this countless times. This will become a valuable faith practice to use not only when you're struggling but all the time.

Some of us allow fear to illuminate our thinking. How many times in this past year have we believed things that will never come to pass? On this day, we can decide to choose faith over fear. It will not be easy, but if we use our energy to believe instead of worry, we will see our thoughts move from the worst-case to the best-case scenario.

I was in Colombia meeting with Sister Valeriana Garcia Martin, who they call Mother Teresa of Colombia. She is in her seventies and has over 150 orphans, all with severe disabilities and special needs. Sister Valeriana provides care and development for these orphans in one of the most impoverished areas of Bogota. She also educates and provides daycare in her school for over 850 children in the community. She considers these children to be her own.

Her orphanage, Hogares Luz y Vida, is translated as Home of Light and Life. Everything she receives is donated, and often, she doesn't know where the donations will come from. There is a constant need for help, as many of the children are medically fragile with severe needs. It would be easy for

Sister Valeriana to look at the overwhelming odds against her and let fear overwhelm her. Yet, when I asked her how she does it all, she said, "I don't know. I just trust God, and He supplies the need. We don't know when or where it's coming from, but God has never failed us." That's faith over fear. I asked what I could do for her to carry this tremendous burden, and she said, "For me, I don't need anything; God will supply all of my needs. Do it for the children. If all we do makes one child smile today, it's been worth it all."

If this simple faith gives her the power to overcome her fear, how can we learn from her example and apply it to our situations? Choosing faith over fear daily will help you not expect the worst but trust for God's best. It will help you find light even in the darkest moment.

What you speak over your life and situation has tremendous power. When fear says, "Your child will never overcome this obstacle," faith says, "All things are possible for those who believe." When fear says, "You've been through too much, you will never be happy," faith says, "I am more than a conqueror through Jesus Christ, and I choose to be happy." When fear says, "You will never make it financially with all you're going through," faith says, "My God shall supply all of my needs according to His riches in glory."

We will always face hills and valleys in our lives. It's what we say about our situation that often stops us on the journey. What you speak will become your reality. Today, encourage yourself by speaking faith over fear.

Pray this: Dear God, I will choose faith over fear no matter what I am going through. I trust that You will guide me every step and that I have nothing to fear. I will trust You in every circumstance and believe that when I do, You will always come through. Amen (So Be It).

Declare this: God has not given me a spirit of fear, so I will declare that my faith will supersede anything that comes against me. I will speak faith words and Scriptures over my life. When I choose faith over fear, I will watch God release a tidal wave of His goodness!

Win for today: Whatever you fear the most today, visualize what success would look like if you conquered that fear. Then, meditate on the success you visualized.

22

Stand

"This is my command—be strong and courageous! Do not be afraid or discouraged. For the Lord your God is with you wherever you go" (Joshua 1:9 NLT).

I recently heard that a study showed standing for 3-4 hours a day is the equivalent of running ten marathons a year. Wow! If this is true, that is solid evidence of the power of a simple activity like standing.

In our spiritual and emotional life, this concept is definitely true. Courage is not by strength; it's by faith. We equate being strong with physical strength. True strength is not physical; it's supernatural. God never asks you to fight; He just wants you to stand. We all have times when we feel surrounded by difficulties and overwhelmed by problems. No matter where we turn, there is no escape. It's easy to get discouraged and think I'll never get out of this. It has me surrounded.

That's how a young servant felt in 2 Kings 6. The king of Aram had just sent a great army with horses and chariots to surround Elisha's house. They snuck up in the middle of the night and had it encircled. The following day, when a young servant went out and saw all the horses and chariots, he nearly passed out. He turned back in total panic.

God must have been saying: Be strong and courageous. Don't be afraid or discouraged; I am with you!

His servant woke up Elisha, "Oh no, my lord! What shall we do?" (2 Kings 6:15 NIV) We're surrounded by the enemy.

Elisha calms the servant, "Don't be afraid. Those who are with us are more than those who are with them" (2 Kings 6:16 NIV).

I can almost hear the servant say: What do you mean, Elisha? It's just you and me. I saw thousands of them. We're about to get slaughtered, and you just want us to stand here?

But Elisha knew the principle in Joshua 1:9, "Be strong and courageous. Do not be afraid; do not be discouraged, for the Lord your God will be with you wherever you go" (NIV). Elisha had already seen that God was fighting for them. He knew this fight was over before it began. They only had to stand there and watch God do it.

2 Kings 6:17 says Elisha prayed, "'Open his eyes, Lord, so that he may see'" (NIV). Suddenly, the young man looked out across the mountainside and saw thousands of warring angels standing beside their chariots of fire, ready to fight.

It reminds me of the story of my friend Nicholas and his family. Nicholas was diagnosed with autism at a young age, but his parents and grandmother believed and hoped that it wouldn't affect him. They would speak hope and positive words into his life. They stood on the Word of God through many trying times and feelings of hopelessness. As a child growing up, many assumed he would never be able to read, write, or do mathematics. Not only did Nick beat the odds, but he also graduated Valedictorian in his high school with a 4.8 grade point average, the highest ever in his school. He received many full-ride scholarships to go to college. He is now becoming everything God created him to be.

Maybe you feel like you are not strong enough to stand today. We all have been there. Even in those times, I found that God has someone near that if you ask, they will support you. God will send someone to stand with you if you are not strong enough alone.

Exodus 17:9 illustrates this beautifully. "So Moses commanded Joshua, 'Choose some men to go out and fight the army of Amalek for us. Tomorrow, I will stand at the top of the hill, holding the staff of God in my hand.' So Joshua did what Moses had commanded and fought the army of Amalek. Meanwhile, Moses, Aaron, and Hur climbed to the top of a nearby hill. As long as Moses held up the staff in his hand, the Israelites had the advantage. But whenever he dropped his hand, the Amalekites gained the advantage. Moses' arms soon became so tired he could no longer hold them up. So Aaron and Hur found a stone for him to sit on. Then they *stood* on each side of Moses, holding up his hands. So his hands held steady until sunset. As a result, Joshua overwhelmed the army of Amalek in battle" (NLT).

I don't know what you are facing today, but God isn't asking you to be a hero or figure it out. He's just asking you to stand on your faith, stand on His Word, stand on the promise, stand in agreement, and watch *Him* do it.

Pray this: Dear God, when I feel like I don't have the strength to figure it out, I know that with Your help, I can stand. You will figure it out and fight for me. I will stand and watch You do it. Amen (So be it).

Declare this: I will stand on God's promises no matter what I face. I am strong and well-able. I have the mind of Christ. I will stand tall with my head held high, knowing I am a child of God.

Win for today: Get help if you're struggling today. Find a mentor or support group to talk to and let them help you. It may be just the encouragement you need to stand strong.

23

If It Ain't Broke, Don't Fix It

"But he said to me, 'My grace is sufficient for you, for my power is made perfect in weakness.' Therefore, I will boast all the more gladly about my weaknesses, so that Christ's power may rest on me" (2 Corinthians 12:9 NIV).

Two vases sit in our home at each side of our front door. One of the vases took a tumble, and the top was broken off. Instead of throwing it away, we carefully put it back together. It may be a little more fragile now, but it's just as beautiful as the other vase. The imperfection is only obvious when you inspect it closely because, though the vase is cracked, it looks and functions exactly as it was designed.

These vases are a daily reminder that just because something is broken doesn't mean it needs to be thrown away. One vase reminds us of a "typical" child, while the other reminds us of a child with special needs. One has a flaw, and one seems normal, but they both have equal value.

Most people would look at a child with special needs as one of very little worth, but God looks at a child with special needs as someone ready to be used.

Scripture beautifully illustrates this in 2 Corinthians 12:9, "But he said to me, 'My grace is sufficient for you, for my power is made perfect in weakness.' Therefore, I will boast all the more gladly of my weaknesses, so that the power of Christ may rest upon me" NIV).

Distressed furniture, which has become popular in recent years, is intentionally made with imperfections. It doesn't take close examination to see that the wood or paint has flaws, but those flaws are what make it so valuable.

God has never created anything that wasn't perfect. Anything that has come out of God's hands was created in His image for a specific purpose.

We, as humans, are the ones who see the imperfections. That's why God tells us in Isaiah 55:8, "My thoughts are not your thoughts, neither are your ways my ways" (NIV). That's why when people come up to special needs parents and say things like, "I'm believing for your son to be made whole," I question, what if he is already whole? What if this was exactly who God created my son to be? Maybe I don't want him "typical." Maybe even with all the struggles, he's brought more meaning and depth to our lives than if we had a typical child. What would you rather experience? A thousand Denny's or one fantastic hole-in-the-wall restaurant with an original menu. I'll take the original.

I've asked myself many times: *Do I want Connor to be fixed, or do I want Connor to be used for God's glory?*

Of course, if my son was healed of autism, that could definitely be used for God's glory, and I believe for the miraculous almost every day. But if Connor never had autism, I don't know if he would be Connor. This is who he is. This is who God created him to be. It might have been easier for our family if he didn't have special needs, but his life has shaped us into who we are. And I love who we are. Scars and all. Bruised and sometimes battered, but still standing. Not victims, but victors!

Sometimes, we look for solutions to temporal problems while God is busy establishing an eternal kingdom. The Bible says in James 4:14, "Yet you do not know what your life will be like tomorrow. For you are just a vapor that appears for a little while, and then vanishes away" (NASB2020). Life on earth is short, and God has minimal time to use us to build His kingdom. We all need relief from difficulties, but I try to remember there are greater things at hand and that our children were created for a much bigger purpose than their diagnosis.

Our children may not have intellectual or physical gifts, but God has given them spiritual gifts. He shines His glory on their gift and surprises us with profound moments.

I will never forget one night I sat with my son at a diner. Connor is in the middle of the spectrum and has difficulty gathering his thoughts to carry on a conversation. Attempting to get him to interact, I asked what he wanted to be when he grew up. Thinking he would give me a standard answer like any child might (a fireman, a singer, a doctor), I was taken aback when suddenly he turned my way and said without hesitation... "Grateful." It was one of the most profound answers that I have ever heard. You wouldn't get that answer from an adult, much less a child. I knew we were in the presence of God, and He was using Connor's spiritual gift to speak through him.

Never underestimate what God can do through a vessel broken to be used. Brokenness has a perfume that pride can never produce.

You see, a vase cannot have a lid. To fulfill its purpose, it must have a hole so it can be poured out. Let me encourage you to leave the crack in your life alone if God allowed it. Maybe it was meant to be there so God could be glorified through it. Don't put a lid on what was meant to be poured out for His purpose.

Pray this: Dear God, I know some areas in my life need to be fixed, but other areas of brokenness hold such beauty. Help me discern what needs to be fixed and what needs to be left alone for Your glory. Amen (So be it).

Declare this: There is *hope* for the future. I trust God with the broken things in my life and believe He will be glorified as our lives are poured out for His purpose.

Win for today: Think of someone disabled and find the beauty in their disability. Ask God to show you how to bring beauty to them.

24
Overflow

"Remember this: Whoever sows sparingly will also reap sparingly, and whoever sows generously will also reap generously. Each of you should give what you have decided in your heart to give, not reluctantly or under compulsion, for God loves a cheerful giver" (2 Corinthians 9:6–8 NIV).

The definition of overflow is the excess or surplus that cannot be accommodated by one available space. What does it take to live in the overflow? We think overflow means having more than enough, and that's true. But overflow doesn't flow from what we receive but from what we give.

When you chase after money and make it your top priority, it will never be enough. You will only become truly prosperous when you live life on purpose and focus on giving of yourself. No person has ever been honored for what he received; honor is bestowed on someone because of how they gave. The happiest people in the world are not those *getting* more but those *giving* more.

To be an overflow person, generosity must be more than a thought—it must be our growth strategy. We have to live a life of generosity. We have to be intentional.

Why are so many people who have all they could want still unhappy? It's usually a matter of the heart.

The rich young ruler reveals this very issue of the heart in Matthew 19:16-22. "Someone came to Jesus with this question: 'Teacher, what good deed must I do to have eternal life?'

'Why ask me about what is good?' Jesus replied. 'There is only One who is good. But to answer your question—if you want to receive eternal life, keep the commandments.'

'Which ones?' the man asked.

And Jesus replied: 'You must not murder. You must not commit adultery. You must not steal. You must not testify falsely. Honor your father and mother. Love your neighbor as yourself.'

'I've obeyed all these commandments,' the young man replied. 'What else must I do?'

Jesus told him, 'If you want to be perfect, go and sell all your possessions and give the money to the poor, and you will have treasure in heaven. Then come, follow me.'

But when the young man heard this, he went away sad, for he had many possessions" (NLT).

What happened in this story? There was a disconnect between the head and the heart. Having a spirit of generosity is difficult when your heart is not in it.

The rich young ruler did all the right things and had all the right answers until it came to the one command his heart couldn't respond to. He had a clogged artery. Luke 6:45 says, "The good person out of the good treasure of his heart produces good, and the evil person out of his evil treasure produces evil, for out of the abundance of the heart his mouth speaks" (ESV).

Here are five keys in Scripture to help you practice the unconditional generosity that triggers overflow in your life.

1. *Don't give personal loans.* Matthew 10:8 says, "Heal the sick, raise the dead, cure those with leprosy, and cast out demons. Give as freely as you have received" (NLT). That means no strings attached! Generosity with strings is not generosity. It's a deal. If you want to live free, give freely.

2. *If you're going through your own storm, be good to someone else.* When you do, you will rise above your storm where the eagles soar. Proverbs 17:17 says, "A friend loves at all times, and a brother is born for adversity" (NKJV). A sincere person not only loves in prosperity but also in adversity.

3. *Do the little extra that most wouldn't do.* Have you ever heard someone say, "You didn't have to do that!" They noticed that you did the little extra that most wouldn't do. Luke 7:44 says, "Then Jesus turned toward the woman and said to Simon, "Do you see this woman? When I came into your house, you gave me no water for my feet, but she washed my feet with her tears and dried them with her hair. You gave me no kiss of greeting, but she has been kissing my feet since I came in. You did not put oil on my head, but she poured perfume on my feet. I tell you that her many sins are forgiven, so she showed great love. But the person who is forgiven only a little will love only a little" (NCV).

4. *Be generous, not for the applause of people, but for the applause of heaven.* Matthew 6:3-4 says, "But when you give to someone in need, don't let your left hand know what your right hand is doing. Give your gifts in private, and your Father, who sees everything, will reward you" (NLT).

5. *Be generous to people that don't deserve it.* This is the ultimate act of

generosity. When Jesus gave His life as a ransom on the cross, He gave His life even though we didn't deserve it. It was the ultimate act of generosity. John 15:13 says, "There is no greater love than to lay down one's life for one's friends" (NLT).

Blake Mycoskie, founder of TOMS, did this very thing. While traveling in Argentina in 2006, Blake witnessed the hardships faced by children growing up without shoes. Wanting to help, he created TOMS, a shoe company that would match every pair of shoes purchased with a new pair for a child in need, called One for One®. What began as a simple idea has evolved into a powerful business model that helps address needs and advance health, education, and economic opportunities for children and their communities. Blake didn't want just to make money. He gave out of a heart of generosity, and God blessed his company. I've found that you will live in the overflow when you do this. Overflow people don't have to give; they *get* to give. They can't help themselves. They breathe generosity. It flows in their veins. They are always looking for someone to be good too.

Overflow people give thanks for ordinary miracles. If you're alive, that's a miracle. If you have food to eat, that's a miracle. If you have a place to live, that's a miracle. Many people around the world don't have those things. When you notice what most people forget every day, you're living in the overflow.

Overflow people walk with a commanded blessing.

When you live in overflow, favor is not something you just receive; favor becomes your identity. When someone sees overflow people, they will call them out by name—there goes "Favor!"

Your generosity activates the Giver of all things. Henri Nouwen says, "God's Kingdom is a place of abundance where every generous act overflows its original bounds and becomes part of the unending grace of God at work in the world."

God dreams that you have an abundance to share with others. 2 Corinthians 9:8 says, "And God will generously provide all you need. Then you will always have everything you need and plenty left over to share with others" (NLT).

It's time to live in the overflow.

Pray this: Dear God, make me an overflow person. Teach me how to give out of a heart of generosity. Your Word says the more I give, the more I will receive. Thank You for making me an overflow person. Amen (So be it).

Declare this: I am an overflow person. I will make a difference in people's lives. I know the more I give, the more God will give back so I can be a blessing to others. His favor surrounds me today!

Win for today: Find someone or something (a nonprofit, ministry, or organization) that you can give your time, talents, or treasure to today. Watch how amazing it will make you feel.

25

Unconditional

"For God so loved the world, that he gave his only Son, that whoever believes in him should not perish but have eternal life" (John 3:16 ESV).

Have you ever been surprised with an extravagant, over-the-top gift? It's surprising because it's uncommon and often given with unconditional love. Unconditional love is rare because it requires sacrifice and is beyond what a human mind can comprehend.

Everything in life today seems so conditional. If you help me with this, I will help you with that. I will loan you money, but you must pay me back with interest. If you love me, then I will love you.

One of the most challenging things in life is to love unconditionally. It's not part of our human nature. Many marriages fall apart because someone's love came with conditions. Friendships that once seemed unbreakable can't be reconciled because trust was broken. Fathers and sons, mothers and daughters, and family units get torn apart over political disagreements, broken promises, and religion. So many can't find a way back because of their differences. Why? Because it doesn't make sense to love extravagantly.

Unconditional love, simply put, is love with no strings attached. It's love you offer freely, a selfless act. It's not based on how much they love you. It's not based on what they can give in return. Simply put, you love them and want nothing more than to see them become everything God created them to be.

This love, called agape love, is the highest form of love. Agape love has the power to unite and heal because it is selfless. It wants nothing in return. John 3:16 says, "For God so loved the world that he gave his one and only Son, that whoever believes in him shall not perish but have eternal life" (NIV). That's extravagant, agape love.

This kind of love might seem like the stuff of fairy tales and movies, not something most people encounter in real life. It's a God kind of love. So why is it so hard to find? Because we are human. Human nature kicks in, and we default to being self-focused.

It's difficult to blame someone who has been deeply wounded for not forgiving their offender. It's logical. It makes sense why we see so many hurting people, hurting people. We think, "You hurt me deeply; you deserve to feel the same hurt."

I'm certainly not here to tell anyone how they should feel or respond in life. I'm not qualified, and I am speaking to the choir myself. I've struggled with offering and receiving forgiveness. I've been given love and, at times, not given it back in the same measure. Oh, how many times have I fallen short?

But I've found that unconditional love is not a one-time encounter. It's nurtured, practiced, and daily inspired by God's love and your time spent with Him. It's a long journey that requires discernment and care.

You can't love someone unconditionally unless your love remains unchanged despite their actions. It doesn't mean you accept abuse and pain or never address situations. Sometimes, acceptance involves recognizing when someone is unlikely to change. In those times, we must put it in God's hands and take steps to protect our well-being, keeping the door open for God to do the miraculous. You may not be able to turn it around, but God can.

We will all come to a divine moment in life when we must choose how to love–with or without conditions. One of the most extraordinary acts of agape, unconditional love is sacrificing something for someone else.

My friend Maxine demonstrated that kind of extravagant, unconditional love. She told me that as a history buff, she always loved restoring old vintage items that were once broken or deemed of no value to their former glory. The process of restoring things is to make them even better than they were before. This is what God did for her.

Father's Day was always painful for Maxine. The relationship with her earthly father was broken due to family pain, trauma, and dysfunction. Despite his drug use and reckless lifestyle, she had shared many special moments with her father. She chose to cling to what was good about him and the moments she cherished.

The last time Maxine saw or heard from her father was at a Greyhound bus stop, where he abandoned her with a small suitcase in her hand. She looked up at him and sobbed, not understanding why he was leaving her there. She was only seven years old.

Somehow, Maxine never stopped praying and believing God would give her another opportunity to see him again. Her love was unconditional.

Earlier this year, while looking for her father, she was able to reconnect with a cousin she found online. Through this cousin, she was able to get her father's number. She was so nervous but worked up the courage to dial the number. The phone rang, but there was no answer. Her husband urged her to leave a message, but she stood there frozen. She had to call back. This time, he picked up the phone.

Maxine had many questions in her heart. Why had he hurt her? Why didn't he want to know her? Thirty-eight years of longing to know about him, but where was he? Why did he leave the way he did?

She felt so much pain and abandonment all of her adult life. However, Maxine said, "The power of the Holy Spirit was so strong that all I could say at the moment was, 'Hi, Dad. It's me – Maxine. I love you.'"

She explained, "The power of forgiveness was so strong; it covered every hurt or pain he could have wielded at me."

"The Lord made it clear to me that this man was broken, saying, 'He could not have loved, cared for, or nurtured you as you needed then, so I restored everything stolen from you. I showed you unconditional love when your father couldn't. I gave you a family and husband that adore you. I did that. I am your Abba Father.'"

Maxine continued, "In that moment, God gave me those words to say to him."

Her dad did not respond right away when he heard her voice. She could only hear a broken, sobbing man on the other line. She knew that God set this precise time for them to reconnect.

Finally, her dad said, "How can you love me? How, after all of these years?

She replied, "Because God loved and forgave me. That's why."

Maxine later said, "This is the God that I serve. He upheld me all of these years. He loved me when my father couldn't, so that's why I was able to love him. I told my dad I graduated college with my bachelor's degree, being the only one in his family to accomplish that. My dad was so proud. It was my greatest gift to reconnect with my dad. I will never forget it."

That's the power of loving unconditionally. This love isn't illusive. It isn't pie in the sky. It isn't out of reach nor relegated to untouchable saints. As Maxine has shown us, it's a real, restorative, life-giving, set-you-free, unconditional kind of love.

I have also been given this mind-blowing, illogical, doesn't-make-sense, unconditional love. God used people to be a gift of His love to me. It was so radical that it changed me more than any other experience in my life. And when I learned to give it back, it changed me even more.

I knew I was on a different playing field after that. It's not where most people play. Most of us might have one foot on that field and one foot out, but we rarely see both feet on God's playing field. Why? Because, humanly speaking, it's way too hard to love unconditionally. You can't do it on your own. It's only when we have the mind and heart of God that He gives us the strength to love unconditionally. It can only be obtained through Him.

You have to pursue this kind of love. Even more, you must let God show you how to be loved. It's hard for us to love others when we can't accept love ourselves. We accept the love we think we deserve. But the truth is, with God, it is not about us deserving His love; it's all about accepting His love. Unconditionally. Only when you receive it can you understand what it means to give it.

Yes, it may cost you something. Loving unconditionally may cost you your pride, but at least it won't cost your family. It may cost you being right, but it won't cost your marriage. It may cost you pleasure, but it won't cost your character.

True love is unconditional.

When our son, Connor, was diagnosed with autism, I remember reading a note in a book by Chuck Colson. After his grandson was diagnosed with autism, a friend sent Chuck a note that said, "Truly, you've been given the greatest gift in having a grandson with special needs. For now, you will understand what it means to unconditionally love."

How true that note was. When your child has special needs, you have to prioritize their needs as a caregiver. Connor has been my greatest gift because he taught me to love unconditionally.

Be unconditional with your love and generosity, and watch God heal your relationships, bring lost children back home, restore your marriage, and bless you beyond your wildest imagination. Heaven will stand in awe when you love like God loves.

Pray this: Dear God, thank You for showing me what unconditional love is. Let Your example inspire me to show unconditional love to others. Your love is extravagant, and I am thankful You love me. Amen (So be it).

Declare this: I will give unconditional, extravagant love. When I give love away, I will get much more in return. My relationships will be stronger, and my life will get better and better. I will forgive more and experience God's forgiveness. I will love more and experience real love in every area of my life.

Win for today: Show someone else the gift of unconditional love in a tangible way. Expect nothing in return. Give it with no strings attached, and watch it bless you.

26

Leave It Better Than You Found It

"Do nothing out of selfish ambition or vain conceit. Rather, in humility value others above yourselves, not looking to your own interests but each of you to the interests of the others" (Philippians 2:3–4 NIV).

Did your parents ever ask you to clean up a mess you didn't make? Once, my co-worker made a huge mess at the office and went home without cleaning it. I told my boss I didn't make the mess, and he said, "Well, someone has to clean it." Even though I didn't make the mess, I was left to clean it up.

This is how we often respond in life. It's not my mess! Why should I have to clean it?

Yet, it's not how you find a mess that matters. It's that you care enough to do something about it.

In the Bible, when the traveler who was beaten and hurt lay on the side of the road, many people passed by even though they could see he was left half dead. Only when the Good Samaritan saw him, stopped, and showed him kindness did we see that his life truly mattered to someone.

I recently saw a video of an experiment in which a man was lying on the ground near a big office building, acting like he was hurt. I watched how many people passed by him without offering help. Several people stared, but many just glanced and ignored him. I was stunned to see how long it took before a good Samaritan finally stopped to help.

I know it may feel easier to avoid the "mess." Maybe we don't have the time or energy to deal with it. But what if your daughter or your son were lying on the road? Would you feel differently?

In the Bible, we see a similar story. Nehemiah was the cupbearer to the king of Persia. Being a cupbearer or a butler for the king was a high-ranking office in the royal courts. It was Nehemiah's duty to ensure any wine served to the king wasn't poisoned. He would ensure the king's safety by drinking some of his wine before serving it. Nehemiah had to be trusted.

Because of his position, Nehemiah learned what it meant to lay down his life for someone. God was about to use him for His glory. Because Nehemiah was willing, God was about to make him a shining light amid devastation and darkness.

I love what Matthew 5:14-16 says about being a light. "You are the light of the world—like a city on a hilltop that cannot be hidden. No one lights a lamp and then puts it under a basket. Instead, a lamp is placed on a stand, where it gives light to everyone in the house. In the same way, let your good deeds shine out for all to see, so that everyone will praise your heavenly Father" (NLT).

To leave something better than you found it, you must be willing to let one thing end so a new thing can begin. It's something greater than yourself. The end of an era is the beginning of a destiny.

In the movie *Saving Private Ryan,* Captain John Miller (Tom Hanks) takes his men behind enemy lines to find Private James Ryan, whose three brothers had been killed in combat. Surrounded by the brutal realities of war while searching for Ryan, each man embarks on a personal journey and discovers their strength to triumph over an uncertain future with honor, decency, and courage. Even though Captain Miller can't save himself, his sacrifice to save Private Ryan leads him to share his dying wish. In one of the most moving scenes, Private Ryan leans into Captain Miller and whispers, "Earn it." Miller was telling Ryan to earn the sacrifices others made so he could go home. In other words, leave it better than you found it.

Decades later, an elderly Ryan and his family visit Miller's grave at the Normandy Cemetery. Ryan says he remembers Miller's words every day, lived his life the best he could, and hopes he has earned their sacrifices.

The moral of the story is to make your life count. Don't let your anointing end with you. Live your life in a way that will deposit something in people that will last.

To leave it better than you found it, your purpose has to be greater than your pleasure. Your concern has to be more important than your comfort.

Nehemiah was the man who cried about a wall. Nehemiah 2:2-3 says, "I was serving the king his wine. I had never before appeared sad in his presence. So the king asked me, 'Why are you looking so sad? You don't look sick to me. You must be deeply troubled.' Then I was terrified, but I replied, 'Long live the king! How can I not be sad? For the city where my ancestors are buried is in ruins, and the gates have been destroyed by fire'" (NLT).

What or who do you cry for? Is a family member going through difficulty? Has a friend suffered some sort of pain? Do you see people who are abused, hungry, or forgotten and need what you have to give? Don't just sit there. Do something about whatever is moving you. God will bless it. God will help you every step of the way.

To leave it better than you found it, don't let the immensity of the need paralyze you from doing the deed. The enemy wants to rock your confidence. People around Nehemiah tried to shake his confidence even though he was trying to do a good thing. You must stand your ground and not let fear of what people might think stop you from your destiny.

Nehemiah stood his ground and said, "But now I said to them, 'You know very well what trouble we are in. Jerusalem lies in ruins, and its gates have been destroyed by fire. Let us rebuild the wall of Jerusalem and end this disgrace!'" (Nehemiah 2:17 NLT)

The enemy believes that if he can steal your confidence, even if you make an effort, the fear of failure will seal your defeat. But Nehemiah's confidence did not lay bare, for it was clothed with the whole armor of God. Nehemiah 2:20 says, "The God of heaven will help us succeed. We, his servants, will start rebuilding this wall" (NLT).

They were determined to leave it better than they found it, and with God's help, they finished it. Nehemiah put to shame all those who doubted him. Nehemiah 6:15-16 says, "So on October 2 the wall was finished—just fifty-two days after we had begun. When our enemies and the surrounding nations heard about it, they were frightened and humiliated. They realized this work had been done with the help of our God" (NLT). People knew God was with Nehemiah and that God had done this.

Amazingly, they not only finished it, but with God on their side, they finished with supersonic speed. That's acceleration. God wants to do it faster than you thought.

When you leave something or someone better than you found it, you leave a mark of faith. God will stamp it, not with an earthly mark, but an eternal mark.

Hebrews 11:1-2 says, "Faith means being sure of the things we hope for and knowing that something is real even if we don't see it. Faith is the reason we remember great people who lived in the past" (NCV).

Be determined to find a way to make a difference in people's lives. It will give you a new perspective on life and profoundly change how you live your own. Release your generosity, and I promise you will fulfill your destiny. A dear friend, Judy Hurst, said it like this, "If you speak from your mind, you will reach a mind; if you speak from your heart, you will reach a heart; if you speak from your life, you will reach a life."

My mother did the most extraordinary thing before she recently passed away. Two years before she passed, she wrote me a letter to find in her Bible after she had died. After experiencing the grief of losing my mom, I can't tell you how much this letter meant to me. It wasn't for me then; it was for me now.

The letter, dated October 1, 2021, said, "Craig, when I'm gone, and we can't share the goodness of God together, I want you to remain strong. Do what God tells you. Walk in the path He shows you. Follow the life map absolutely; keep an eye out for the signposts. God has a course for your life, and as long as you hold onto His nail-scared hands, you will do well in whatever you do and wherever you go. Continue to remain humble before God. He has you in the palm of His hands. He will never let you fall. Always remember how much I loved you and prayed for you. I feel I will be in that cloud of witnesses rooting you on to the finishing line."

It was a love letter from heaven.

What was she saying? Craig, earn it. Put God first and leave it better than you found it. Finish well so others can finish well through your example. This is called passing the torch of legacy and paying it forward.

Nehemiah is saying something powerful to us today. What do you cry for? Who needs what you have to give? Where can you make a difference for those who come after you? Please don't wait for someone to do it. Don't let others talk you out of it. Choose today to leave it better than you found it.

Pray this: Dear God, Your Word says the harvest is plentiful, but the workers are few. Let me be one of the few to leave this world better than I found it. Please use me to make a difference and leave a legacy. Amen (So be it).

Declare this: I will leave a legacy. I will lift the fallen, help the broken, and make a difference in someone's life every chance I am able. I want to finish well and leave this world better than I found it.

Win for today: Think about what has been tugging on your heart recently. What do you feel moved by? Take an action step to respond to that need. Leave it better than you found it.

27

How To Hear the Voice of God

"Call to me and I will answer you and tell you great and unsearchable things you do not know" (Jeremiah 33:3).

I have been asked many times how to hear God's voice. My response is always the same: It depends on who holds your devotion.

Devotion means loyalty, love, or care for someone or something; it is a deep commitment. When you have a devotional life with God, you will grow spiritually and be on the same page as Him. Why? Because you are devoting yourself to a relationship with Him. You get to know God. You have a sense of how He speaks to you.

God created us to be in relationship with him. But how can you know God if you don't spend time with Him? The same is true in a marriage. What kind of relationship would you have if you only talked to your spouse when you needed something? Your relationship would be one-sided and not very good. You must spend time with your spouse to have a meaningful relationship with them. You talk to them daily; you want to please them and find out what you can do to build the best relationship. When you do, you will see the investment pay off and last.

Devotion to God helps us remember that no matter what is happening in the world, God is in control. He's got us and holds our world in the palm of His hands.

What are the keys to having a consistent devotional life and hearing God's voice?

Make it a daily priority! When battling through challenges, there's nothing more important than having a daily relationship with God. We all experience the ups and downs of life. One day is great, but the next day difficulty hits. How do you find stability regardless of your circumstances? We must have God's direction. We must be able to hear Him speak.

Romans 3:16-17 says, "All Scripture is breathed out by God and profitable for teaching, for reproof, for correction, and for training in righteousness, that the man of God may be complete, equipped for every good work" (ESV).

To build a thriving devotional life, making time every day is essential. It's a discipline that will likely start small and grow in time. Start with the first 15 minutes of the day. Then, as you grow stronger, you might spend 30 minutes or an hour a day. I started with 15 minutes, but as I spent time with God consistently, I craved more time with Him. You will find the more you get from Jesus, the more you want. There will come a time when you can't go a day without Him.

I love that Jesus modeled a devotional life when he lived as a human being on earth. He displayed how vital His devotional life was between Him and His Father. Jesus would go early in the morning to meditate and spend time in prayer. Mark 1:35 says, "In the early morning, while it was still dark, Jesus got up, left the house, and went away to a secluded place, and was praying there" (NASB 1995).

Anytime is a good time to pray. But Jesus must have felt it important to start His day hearing from His Father. You might say, I'm not an early riser; can I do it at night? Absolutely! God is pleased with whatever time you spend with Him. If you want to follow His example, though, start at the beginning of your day. Starting the morning in prayer greatly impacts how you respond and look at the day. As you consistently spend time with God, you will gain momentum.

God has spoken to me countless times and in unique ways during my devotional time. In my experience, though, God speaks most consistently through His Word. The Bible is God speaking. If you don't read it, you will struggle to hear Him speak. The more time you spend studying and reflecting on God's word, the more you will understand what He is saying.

God speaks through reminders. When Jesus ate with his disciples before he was crucified, the Bible says He broke the bread and said, "This is my body which was broken for you; do this in remembrance of me" (1 Corinthians 11:24 NKJV). He wanted them to remember His sacrifice whenever they failed. These reminders from God bring us peace in the middle of our storms. Since He is called the Prince of Peace, who better to turn to when you need peace of mind. If you don't have peace today, find Scriptures about peace and quote them throughout the day. When you quote Scripture, you are reminding yourself of what God says. Doing this myself, I have often felt an incredible sense of peace that everything will be okay. God is speaking through His Word.

He can also speak through other people. Romans 12:6-8 says, "In his grace, God has given us different gifts for doing certain things well. So, if

God has given you the ability to prophesy, speak out with as much faith as God has given you. If your gift is serving others, serve them well. If you are a teacher, teach well. If your gift is to encourage others, be encouraging. If it is giving, give generously. If God has given you leadership ability, take the responsibility seriously. And if you have a gift for showing kindness to others, do it gladly" (NLT). God definitely uses people to speak. But, I encourage you not to depend on people entirely for God to speak to you. Learn to hear His voice yourself, and allow Him to speak in multiple ways.

I've found that God can speak through His assurances. Genuine assurance can only come from a Heavenly Father who loves you. Like when you made a mistake as a child and thought it was the end of the world until your daddy hugged you and said, "Don't worry. Everything will be alright." God longs to assure us in the same way. As the song "Blessed Assurance" says, "Blessed assurance, Jesus is mine. Oh, what a foretaste of glory divine." When Jesus is ours, we have an assurance of what's coming. We have the assurance that He has done it before and will do it again. Reminders and assurances are a powerful way to hear God speak.

God can speak through His creation. When you see the magnificent sky or the beautiful sunrise, God is saying to you, "Is anything too great for Me?"

He speaks through humility. When you feel humbled by a situation, know that God is speaking and leading you to a better way.

God speaks through gratitude. Have you ever been overwhelmed with gratitude, knowing only God could have accomplished something? Has He been so good that you start to get emotional and thank Him? Take time to listen for Him in those moments. You may hear God in your thoughts, saying, "I'm so proud of you. I love you so much! You are my child." I've heard God's voice many times in moments of gratitude.

Another critical way we hear the voice of God is through His promises, especially when we face difficult times. I've heard God speak through my pain. He reassures me that the Bible says His promises are "yes and amen" (2 Corinthians 1:20 NKJV). I hold on to the promises He has spoken over me. David said in Psalm 119:49-50, "Remember your word to your servant, in which you have made me hope. This is my comfort in my affliction, that your promise gives me life" (ESV). God is faithful to His word. When He promises you something, He will do it.

You can also hear God speak through the Holy Spirit. John 14:26 says, "But when the Father sends the Advocate as my representative—that is, the

Holy Spirit—he will teach you everything and will remind you of everything I have told you" (NLT). The two primary ways the Holy Spirit speaks to us are through discernment and by teaching us what to do and what not to do. One way I think of the Holy Spirit is as my conscience. He will convict me when I'm wrong and direct me when I'm headed in the right direction. Even Jesus was led by the Holy Spirit. If we listen, the Holy Spirit is an excellent communicator of what God wants.

Lastly, God speaks through your praise and worship to Him. In 2 Chronicles 20, we read about three armies about to attack Israel. King Jehoshaphat knows that these armies will wipe him out. Have you ever felt like somebody was going to wipe you out? Perhaps you've felt like your addiction, illness, or circumstance would take you out. This is how the entire nation of Israel felt. They felt hopeless and without a chance.

In the natural, they didn't have a chance to win against these armies. But suddenly, a man in the middle of the crowd spoke out and said, "The battle is not yours, but God's" (2 Chronicles 20:15 NIV). Now, *that* was a declaration! God never gives a declaration without a plan.

The man continues giving instructions from God: Here's what I want you to do. Go to where you're supposed to fight. Give Me praise, glory, and honor. Then, stand there and watch Me do it.

In other words - Go and sit at My feet. That's how you offer praise, glory, and honor. I want you to receive from Me and watch Me move in your situation. Here comes the victory!

That's precisely what the Israelites did. It was amazing! One army started fighting another, then another, while the Israelites stood and watched. They probably didn't fully know why, but the armies fought each other until all three were wiped out.

Not only did the Israelites win the battle, but they carried back more plunder than they could contain. And, just as God promised, King Jehoshaphat didn't have to lift a finger. We don't have to fight alone.

Are you fighting battles you were never meant to fight? Put Jesus first and learn to hear His voice. I attribute every victory I've experienced to seeking God and being open to hearing His voice.

There are many ways God will speak. The question is, are you listening? Take these tools and remain open to how God speaks to you. Apply them in your daily walk, make them daily habits, and you will hear God's voice speak to you.

Pray this: Dear God, I know you speak to me in many ways. Let me be open to hearing your voice and put myself in a position to hear you speak every day. Amen (So be it).

Declare this: I will go after God by spending time with God. I will look for ways to allow God to speak to me. As God speaks, I will follow his direction and fulfill my destiny.

Win for today: Take five minutes to pray and ten minutes to allow God to speak to you.

28

No Two Journeys Are the Same

"A brother offended is more unyielding than a strong city, and quarreling is like the bars of a castle" (Proverbs 18:19 ESV).

A culture of grace will never exist when we are unwilling to go the extra mile to extend grace without judgment. This scripture in Proverbs powerfully states that when we are offended, we are as unyielding as a strong city. We become like a prison with bars.

When someone is not like us, it's difficult to see past our differences. When we focus on those differences, we fail to convey the grace and love needed to bring hope and healing.

Today, because of the human condition, we continue to struggle with racial barriers, socioeconomic class wars, and stigmas based on our looks, abilities, and status. These stigmas are often passed down like a generational curse for the next person to inherit. Nothing is more infuriating than a presumably mature parent passing down an ignorant, uneducated thought to an immature child. But, as believers, it's important to offer the same grace to others as we ask people to offer us. We can either hold an offense or try to understand what ill-informed thought has been passed down to them. If we were ingrained with the same ideology by our parents and community, how difficult would it be for us to look at things differently?

I've seen many special needs parents, including myself, hold an offense by how our child was treated. We want everyone to understand our journey, but no two journeys are alike. There comes a time when, after we've done what we can, we must let go and trust God to change hearts.

If you've been discriminated against based on race, ethnicity, socioeconomic status, or any social justice issue, it can be incredibly hurtful and frustrating. Once that seed of offense has taken root, it's difficult to pull it out. If you let the offense grow, it will make you bitter. Once you're bitter, it's tough to get better. You may have a noble cause and be justified in how you feel, but unresolved pain causes us to live a sad, hurt, and angry life.

Two scriptures in the Bible that spell out this truth woke me up. Ephesians

4:31 says, "Let all bitterness and wrath and anger and clamor and slander be put away from you, along with all malice" (NASB1995). Furthermore, Matthew 6:15 says, "But if you do not forgive others their trespasses, neither will your Father forgive your trespasses" (NKJV). Wow! That's a difficult truth to accept when you've been deeply hurt by something or someone.

My friend Karl Hagestrom asked me to speak about special needs at a crusade in Africa. Thousands of people came from across the valley to hear about a God who loves them. I was very excited to speak! As I was waiting to go on stage, Karl leaned over and said, "You know, I'm not sure how these people will respond to your message tonight. You must understand there is a huge negative stigma concerning those with special needs. They think their children are cursed."

Immediately, righteous indignation rose within me, and I thought to myself, "I will tell them! I'll set them straight! How can these people look at these children as a curse!?"

Just then, one of the interns with us said, "Yes, even here at the crusade, it's freaking us out a little bit. They are bringing kids who have special needs into the prayer tent and asking us to cast the demons out of these children when we know they are just children with special needs. We are trying to explain to parents that their children don't have demons; they have challenges."

My mind was blown. Do they think their children are demon-possessed when they only have special needs? What is wrong with these people!?

This is a horrible stigma in many third-world countries. In some tribes, special needs children are hidden because they are considered a curse upon the family. Their children may even be killed. A leader who works for this organization in Africa explained that parents would tie a rope around a brick, attach it to the child's ankle, and throw the child in a lake to drown.

I thought to myself, "What is the matter with these people? How can they think this way!?"

In most third-world countries, special needs children aren't allowed to attend school, church, or be seen in public places. These children carry the stigma of being cursed, and "normal" people don't want to be around them. Even kids with AIDS can go to school and church in Africa, but children with special needs are forbidden.

I saw this very thing when I visited Kenya. A little girl with autism wanted to go to school so badly that she would walk there with her cousin. Not allowed inside, she would sit outside alone while her cousin was learning in the classroom. When we drove up to the school, this little girl had the biggest smile as she greeted our team. Her smile could brighten any room. She would sit outside for hours, waiting for her cousin to finish school until it was time to go home. Despite her commitment, she was never allowed the same privileges other children were given.

At that moment, I didn't want to understand why people felt this way. I wanted to tell them how wrong they were. How could they reject a child this way!?

Now, sitting at this crusade, I became a little nervous when Karl and the interns told me these things. There were no barriers between the stage and the people. If I said the wrong thing, I could be in big trouble. I began to pray silently, "God, I know I am supposed to be here. I know You are using me, and others like me, to break down stigmas and allow Your grace to bring awareness and hope to special needs families. Please let me give them the same grace You've given me."

That night, I took the stage and spoke a bold message: "Your children with special needs are not a curse; they are a blessing. God will use your special needs children to do great things." I explained why those with special needs were important to God and why they should matter to us.

People didn't respond to my message with a roar of approval, but at least they didn't chase me off the stage. You could tell they had never heard anyone say that a child with special needs was a gift, not a burden. Many lives were impacted. We had parents tell us how much they loved their special needs child, but they had only been taught what was wrong with their child, not what was right.

I realized something that day. *As limited as awareness can be about the value of special needs children around the world, everyone is on a different journey.*

Just because someone doesn't know how to respond to a special needs child doesn't mean they can't learn. They don't have to stay ignorant for life. We must have the fortitude to let go of offense and discern where people are in their understanding. We must consider how we can teach them and bring them along on their journey.

Ignorance is taught and caught. So is tolerance. But you can't fight ignorance with intolerance. The more we try to understand each person or culture's journey, the more effective we'll be at bringing awareness. We want others to feel injustice like we do. But if they haven't walked in our shoes, they can't fully understand what we have walked through. We can get mad and bitter and judge them. Or, we can teach, bring awareness, pray, and trust God to change them.

1 Corinthians 13:7 talks about the importance of loving, especially while carrying an offense. It says, "Love bears all things, believes all things, hopes all things, endures all things" (ESV). This scripture reminds us that when we truly love, it will be shown by our ability to bear with one another even when we are hurt. We should remain steadfast and hopeful, even in the face of offense. Is it easy? No, it's really hard. Yet, God would never ask us to do something He wouldn't do.

I heard someone say, "I never worry about how others treat me; I only worry about how I treat others." We can't control how others think or feel. We can only control how we think or feel about others. We may never understand others in life, but our pursuit should be to bring understanding. No two journeys are the same.

Pray this: Dear God, please give me the discernment and understanding to know where people are and the grace to help them in their journey. I know only You can change hearts, so help me not to judge even when I may be right. You will bring healing and hope when I trust You to do it. Amen (So be it).

Declare this: I believe God is able to do exceedingly and abundantly more than I can ask, think, or imagine, even in hard situations. I will live as a healer and let God do the healing. I will not get bitter when I don't understand, but I will understand better through God's love and guidance.

Win for today: Pray for someone who has hurt you. Ask God to change their heart. Take the high road and watch God heal the broken road you've walked on.

29
Not So Ordinary Miracles

"Make thankfulness your sacrifice to God and keep the vows you made to the Most High. Then call on me when you are in trouble, and I will rescue you, and you will give me glory" (Psalm 50:14–15 NLT).

A child playing with friends, a little girl talking to her mother, a middle school boy going to the bathroom alone, a father and son playing catch… These simple actions may seem ordinary to some. To others, they would be a miracle. Amazingly, the human mind is conditioned to believe what is ordinary and what is a miracle.

Like most kids, our son Connor said his first words when he was around one year old. He was a chatterbox for the next year until he turned two, which was somewhat normal to us. Our other two children, Cory and Courtney, who are 10 and 12 years older than Connor, were the same way. They talked incessantly.

At a very young age, my son Cory loved to watch a *Super Book* video about David and Goliath. He walked around the house, swinging a plastic sword and cloth sling, declaring, "I will slay you Gowiath (Goliath) in the name of the Loward (Lord), for Him is on my side!" After throwing an imaginary stone, he would run over and knock down a toy transformer. Then, with a mighty swing of his sword, Cory cut off the transformer's head. (Which we had to tape back over and over.) He would then proclaim as he held the transformer's head in his hand, "God has dewivered this Philwistine into my hand!" I don't know how biblically correct this was, but watching him do it was hilarious.

This is normal, right? Every kid does this.

Fast-forward to when my son Connor was two years old. He went from speaking freely and saying "I love you" without hesitation to suddenly saying nothing. He had always played well with other kids, but now, he would sit in a corner and only play alone. Seemingly overnight, we lost who Connor had been. For the next three years, we would barely hear our son put two words together. What had once been ordinary would now become a miracle.

It's interesting what we take for granted in life because it happens so naturally or shows up in abundance. I remember the first hurricane I experienced after coming to Houston. When the 100 mph winds and rain finally stopped, there was no electricity or running water for multiple days. In an instant, utilities that seemed so ordinary a few days prior became scarce.

The truth is that life is a miracle. Miracles happen around us every day. The very things we take for granted because they come effortlessly would become miracles if taken away. No one understands that more than a special needs parent.

When you were preparing with joy and excitement to have your new baby, you must have dreamed about everything they would do. But it didn't turn out that way. God had a scarier, bigger plan. You thought your child would do ordinary things like other kids, but instead, God allowed you to see miracles no one else can see, like a blind spot coming into full view.

For instance, most people in America can ask for a drink of clean or bottled water. It seems like an ordinary request, right? Yet, it would be a not-so-ordinary miracle for a child in Africa, where they only have access to dirty and diseased water.

Most parents can expect to have a healthy child outside of the occasional cold or flu. Yet, this would be an extraordinary miracle to my friend and blogger Barb Dittrich, who has seen her children in and out of hospitals for years. A little girl talking to her mom seems pretty ordinary to many parents. But for my wife and me, to hear one sentence from our son after years of silence would be beyond a miracle.

For three years, we barely heard Connor speak. He would point to things he needed. Because he couldn't speak, he would get frustrated and act out. Sometimes, he would have terrible fits. Other times, he would bite or scratch his arms. I remember one day, driving to work, I asked God why. I wasn't asking God why I had my son; I was asking God why my son is not able to speak. Why does he have to struggle so much in frustration? I'll never forget what God spoke to me in my spirit. God said, "Your child is not a burden. Your child is a gift."

I said, "I know what you mean, God. He's our son. We love him, and of course, he's a gift. But do You see how much he's struggling?"

God said it again, "Your child is not a burden. Your child is a gift. You are looking at the struggle and not seeing how I can use your test and make it a testimony. I am going to use your son to reach millions of people."

"Are you kidding me, God? How is my son going to reach millions of people? Right now, he can't even ask for a drink of water?"

Then God spoke four words that He says to those in the desert.

He said, "Do you trust me?"

I gave God a very simple and vulnerable answer. "You are all we've got in this situation. There is no cure for autism but You. *We trust You.*"

God later said to me, "Thank Me for the miracles I am already doing, every day, all around you, and watch me do the miracles yet to be seen. Your son is alive; that's a miracle. Those who can't have children would be so proud to have a son like Connor. Your son gives you a hug and a kiss when you ask. That's a miracle. Many autistic children don't do that. Thank Me for the not-so-ordinary miracles, and watch Me surprise you with My goodness."

You would think life got easier after hearing God speak like that, right? It didn't. It got worse. After God speaks, He often wants to see if we will trust Him and be grateful for what He's said. Praise precedes the victory.

About three months later, as my wife, Sam, was putting our son to bed, she started yelling, "Craig, Craig, get up here! Hurry!"

I quickly ran upstairs into my son's room and asked, "What is the matter?"

Sam said, "I was putting Connor to bed, reading a book, and praying with him. As I turned off the light, he suddenly began to speak. One word after another word, one sentence after another sentence."

I said, "You have got to be kidding me. What...what did he say?"

Sam walked me over to his bed and said, "Connor, say it again. Say it for Daddy."

He lifted his head and, in broken English, began to speak. "This is my Bible. I am what it says I am. I have what it says I have. I can do what it says I can do. Tonight, I will be taught the Word of God. I boldly confess, my mind is alert, my heart is receptive, I will never be the same. I am about to receive the incorruptible, indestructible, ever-living seed of the Word of God. I will never be the same. Never, never, never. I will never be the same in Jesus' name. Amen."

Those were the first sentences we heard our son speak in three years. To say we were overwhelmed would be an understatement. We were crying, hugging, jumping, and yelling! We called everyone we knew and videotaped Connor saying the "This Is My Bible" pledge. Now, millions of people have heard that testimony. It has been written about in nine books and inspired the launch of Champions Club developmental centers for special needs kids around the world.

God showed us something powerful through all of this. Try not to look at the burden; focus on the gift. Celebrate what we *do* have, not what we don't. We have so much to be grateful for, even despite our challenges. Someone in a more challenging situation would trade places with us in a heartbeat.

Lastly, begin to notice the not-so-ordinary miracles happening every day. What one may see as ordinary, another may see as a miracle. When you notice that God is doing miracles all around you, the ordinary becomes extraordinary.

Pray this: Dear God, I will look for the extraordinary in everything. I know You show us the simplest things are the most beautiful things. Let me see You at work, in both big and small ways. Amen (So be it).

Declare this: I will look for and appreciate the ordinary miracles in my life and then watch You do the extraordinary miracles in my life. My best days are ahead. New miracles are coming my way. Thank you, God, that you will surprise me with Your goodness today!

Win for today: Name five ordinary miracles God does for you every day. Then, ask Him to do an extraordinary miracle you have never seen before.

30

Do You Know Who You Are?

"For you created my inmost being; you knit me together in my mother's womb. I praise you because I am fearfully and wonderfully made; your works are wonderful, I know that full well" (Psalm 139:13–14 NIV).

On this journey, knowing our identity in Christ is vital. The enemy would love nothing more than for us to lose our identity. We so easily get wrapped up in another person or thing, trying to become like them, that we lose sight of who we are. Often, it's because we don't like much about ourselves. We're so insecure about our looks, jobs, and lives that we try to be someone else. We have let our fears turn us into someone we never wanted to be. Our fears shouldn't define us; our faith should. I think so many of us live in fear of what is next. When we're afraid, it's easy to forget who we are. The enemy wants us to forget who we are and Whose we are. Yet, God has uniquely created us for a specific purpose.

The other day, I donated blood at a donor bank. When donating, they ask for your blood type to match your blood with a recipient of the same type. Because I gave blood, now one lucky person will wake up from an operation with a sudden craving for Captain Crunch & the ability to quote key lines from the movie Star Wars.

The point is that your identity unlocks opportunity.

Carrying a driver's license allows us to cash a check, enter an event, and drive to where we want to go without fear of being stopped. Without identity, we are limited. When we accept Jesus into our hearts, we have a new identity that comes with benefits. We become VIP's. A personal relationship with God allows us to go places we never thought possible.

If you don't know who you are, somebody will tell you who *they* think you should be. Maybe you've relied too much on an identity someone else has given you. Family, friends, doctors, educators, and even strangers will tell you who you need to be. Our challenges, fears, and worries love to define us. Perhaps you don't know your true identity because you've allowed other voices to speak louder than you've allowed God's voice into your life.

Don't be too hard on yourself. We all have. But maybe it's time to quit depending on others for approval and start depending on God's approval. If we let God define us instead of our circumstances, we may see ourselves in a different light.

You've got to know who you are and Whose you are, then speak it over yourself daily. Every day, get up and say, "I am talented, amazing, a masterpiece." If you have children, say, "My child is talented, important, and beautiful." When you say those things, you recognize who you are in Christ.

When you speak negative words about yourself, you are repeating what someone else has spoken over you. You're taking on their identity, not your own. Only God knows who you are. You have His DNA inside of you. You are a prince or princess of the King.

Don't let people label you. Throughout life, people frequently stick labels on us, telling us what we can and cannot become. Sometimes this is a good thing. People speak faith into us. They encourage us. Other times, people put negative labels on us. You cannot stop the discouraging comments or prevent the negative labels, but you can choose to remove them.

As a teenager, Walt Disney was told by his art instructor that he wasn't creative and had no imagination. Disney was smart enough to remove that label. He went on to do pretty well. Lucille Ball, the comedian and actress, was told she had no acting skills and should try a different profession. She removed that label. Winston Churchill failed the sixth grade. He was told he wasn't smart enough. He went on to become one of the greatest Prime Ministers that ever lived. Helen Keller was told she was a throwaway and wouldn't amount to anything in life because she was deaf, mute, and blind. However, she got multiple degrees and became an icon of hope for those with special needs.

The common denominator in the success of these people is that they chose to remove the negative labels. You can do the same today. Don't let people label you. They don't determine your lot in life. Don't focus on what others say; focus on what God says. Don't look at your problems; look at your Problem Solver.

Have you stuck a label on yourself because of your circumstances? Have you stopped dreaming? Take that label off. Start believing again that you were made for more. Yes, life may look different, and the path may be harder, but God didn't create you just to squelch your dreams. Only we can stop our dreams from happening. He will give you strength and help you accomplish your goals.

Take the labels off of you and your family. Know who you are in Christ. Believe who He says you are. *Be all of who God has created you to be.*

The world is suffering from an identity crisis.

I heard a story of a pastor who was approached by a young woman after service. She had two small children with her, a girl and a boy. They were so loving. The little boy, about five years old, hung on to the pastor and didn't want to let go. The pastor hugged him back, and they talked for a little while. Finally, the pastor high-fived the little boy, and the family walked away. A few minutes later, the boy returned to whisper something in the pastor's ear. The pastor leaned down and would never forget what the little boy said. "I wish you were my dad." That almost broke the pastor's heart. The pastor told him what I'm telling you: Every morning, look up and imagine your heavenly Father is smiling down on you. He's saying, "You're the apple of My eye. You're My most prized possession." Scripture says God will be a Father to the fatherless (Psalm 68:5 NIV).

Because many people lack their identity, they are not reaching their full potential. Their minds are full of thoughts saying, "You're not from the right family." "You don't even have a father. No wonder you can't succeed." Don't believe those lies. Believe this instead: "I am who God says I am. I may not have an earthly father, but I have a heavenly Father. People may have spoken negatively about me, but God blessed me before anyone could curse me. That's what I'm going to dwell on."

If the negative things spoken over you are poisoning your future, return to the roots of those thoughts. Detox that garbage. Detox what your ex-husband said about you. Detox what that teacher said you couldn't do. Detox what that manager said you would never become. Detox what those critics said about your ability.

Pray this: Dear God, thank you that my identity is in You. I can take off the labels and be who You say I am. I am a child of God made with royal blood flowing through my veins. I have your DNA of greatness. I receive it today. Amen (So be it).

Declare this: I am more than a conqueror. I can do all things through Christ. I am a victor and never a victim. I am the head and not the tail. I am above and not beneath. I will do great things in life. This is my identity!

Win for today: Write down three things you love about yourself. Next, write down three things God says about you. Then, write down three things you want to become. Speak those nine things over your life all day. Let it shape your identity today.

31

Stop Renting, Start Owning

"I have given you a land for which you did not labor, and cities which you did not build, and you dwell in them; you eat of the vineyards and olive groves which you did not plant" (Joshua 24:13 NKJV).

During high school graduation, nobody ever says, "I can't wait to go to college, work hard, and get a degree so I can rent someday." Have you ever wondered how we talk to teenagers about cleaning their rooms and doing the dishes? It's like talking to the walking dead; they don't get it. Our kids keep their rooms a mess because they don't own them. If a cost was involved, it might influence how they took care of their belongings and responsibilities.

Many times, we do the exact same thing in our spiritual life. We rent God's Word rather than own it. We don't speak from victory. We speak to victory.

I recently researched the difference between renting and owning a property. Both ownership and renting can have benefits, but there is a big distinction between the two. Below are a few results of the comparison.

The benefits of renting are (1) less commitment, (2) it's easier to move on, and (3) someone else does the work. When renting, you are not planted in your home. Since you're not tied down, you can move quickly. You don't have to be committed to your neighbors or community. Best of all, you aren't responsible for property taxes or insurance, and someone else handles the maintenance and upkeep.

In contrast, the benefits of owning are (1) building equity, (2) leaving an inheritance, (3) getting a return on your investment, and (4) living in community with others. When you own, your monthly housing cost builds equity. Usually, the more you pour in, the more you will get out. You will also have something to pass down as an inheritance for your family. Owners can make a return on their investment by making home improvements and deducting taxes at the end of the year. Finally, ownership allows you to build community with your neighbors. When you're part of a community, people have your back.

If ownership has such meaningful benefits, why do we keep ourselves in a position of renting?

The same principle applies to our spiritual lives. God never intended for us to be renters of his favor, renters of His Word, or renters of His promises. He called us to *own* His Word and promises.

Don't just rent the house; own the house. Don't just rent our relationships; own our relationships. Don't just rent your dreams; own your dreams.

I read about a famous engineer who did just that. The story explains, "Between Austria and Italy, there is a section of the Alps where it is an impossibly steep, very high part of the mountains. This engineer built a train track over these Alps to connect Vienna and Venice. He built these tracks even before there was a train in existence that could make the trip. He built it because he knew some day, the train would come." Indeed, the train did come. That's what I call taking ownership of a dream. Wow!

I love what Clint Eastwood, the famous actor and director, said at 91 when his partner asked, "How old are you, Clint?"

"I turn 91 on Monday," Clint replied.

"What are you going to do?" the partner asked.

"I am going to start a new movie," Clint casually replied.

Surprised, the partner asked, "What keeps you going?"

Clint wisely responded, "I get up every day and don't let the old man in." That's an owner's mentality. At 91, Clint refuses to let the old man into his house. I love that!

In 2003, the fate of British Cycling took a turn. At the time, the sport had endured nearly 100 years of mediocrity. Since 1908, British riders had only won a single medal in the Olympics and had never won a Tour de France in its 110-year existence until a guy named Dave Beresford was hired.

Dave developed the strategy of aggregating marginal gains, which is the philosophy of searching for a tiny margin of improvement in everything you do. First, they redesigned the bike seats to make them more comfortable. Next, they asked riders to wear electronically heated over-shorts to maintain an ideal temperature while riding. They stayed focused on making 1% improvements.

Only five years after Beresford took over, the British Cycling team dominated the Beijing Olympic Games, winning an astounding 60% of the gold medals. Four years later, in the next Olympic Games, they set nine Olympic records and seven world records. That same year, Bradley Wiggins became the first British Cyclist to win the Tour de France.

What happened? They consistently made small deposits and changed their mentality from renting to owning.

When you know God has promised you greater things, you don't wait for a sign to appear before you respond. If you don't move, God won't move. Right now, you don't need to have enough faith to finish. You just need enough faith to start. It's time for ownership. You've been renting long enough. Are you willing to lay down some track before your miracle arrives? That's taking ownership.

People's lives are hanging in the balance.

Just imagine what would have happened if Jesus "rented" the cross. The Bible says he could have called legions of angels down from Heaven, but he wasn't a renter of the cross, the pain, or the sacrifice. He was an owner. And because He owned it, we are guaranteed to live in Heaven forever when we ask Jesus into our hearts.

You will struggle to fulfill your destiny as long as you live in a renter or get-by mentality. When facing challenges, there comes a point where, even if *you* are unsure, you still have confidence that *God* can overcome them. You can't, but God can! This faith shifts you from renting God's promises to owning God's promises.

The Bible says in Psalm 50:10, "All the animals of the forest are mine, and I own the cattle on a thousand hills" (NLT). God owns it all, and you are His child. If you will own it, you will receive your inheritance.

Pray this: Dear God, You are my father and provider. I receive Your inheritance today. I will take ownership of all You desire for me to have. I will give You all the glory for the provision. Amen (So be it).

Declare this: I refuse to have a renter's mentality. I will own God's Word. I will own His promises. I will walk in His favor as a child of the Most High God. I am taking ownership of my inheritance.

Win for today: List five promises God has given you. Find five promises in Scripture that match the promises God gave you. Start today by praying over the promises from His Word.

Made in the USA
Middletown, DE
13 November 2024